A EUROPEAN RECOVERY PROGRAMME

A EUROPEAN RECOVERY PROGRAMME

Restoring Full Employment

edited by

Ken Coates MEP & Michael Barratt Brown

SPOKESMAN
for
EUROPEAN LABOUR FORUM

First published in Great Britain in 1993 by
Spokesman
Bertrand Russell House
Gamble Street
Nottingham, England
Tel. 0602 708318

Copyright ©Spokesman, 1993

British Library Cataloguing in Publication Data available on request
ISBN 0-85124-539-0 cloth
ISBN 0-85124-549-8 paper

Printed by the Russell Press Ltd, Nottingham
(Tel. 0602 784505)

CONTENTS

CHAPTER 1

The Spectre of Unemployment

Ken Coates MEP

A spectre is haunting Europe. It is the shadow of unemployment. The present figures are quite dreadful, and have created desperate social tensions in many areas. But the situation today, even while we are caught in the depths of slump, is nothing like as bad as the forecast of what is to come.

Here is the problem: there has been a tremendous improvement in production technologies, as the result of applied electronics. New machines are labour saving to the nth degree. The slump has slowed investment, which means that older technologies have been able to hang on just that little bit longer. Any "recovery" will, however, see a rush to buy newer and better machines, which will actually increase the numbers of people in the dole queues. True, in theory, if the economy expanded very rapidly, new industries might generate brand-new jobs to begin to staunch the wounds. But we are told by the analysts that this is almost certainly not going to happen.

The world debt crisis will mean that Europe will have to sell to itself and a handful of developed nations. Without immense programmes of redistribution, Latin America, Africa and the poorer parts of Asia will not exist as customers. So "recovery" means very modest growth, but very rapid increases in unemployment.

The best guess is that there will be 12.5 per cent unemployment throughout the European Community by the end of the century. Large parts of the Third World, especially in Latin America, will be suffering unemployment of between 40 and 50 per cent. In Russia and most of Eastern Europe they will be very fortunate to avoid a 20 per cent level.

All this is a recipe for disaster. Crisis on this scale touches all around it. We are bound to doubt whether the social fabric can take the strain of such misery and distress.

Never forget that youth unemployment runs at something like double the general rate. Already disaffected young people, in several countries, are joining in racist attacks on immigrants, or voting for extremist parties of the right. If we all sit and do nothing, we can expect to witness shocking sights in our streets, as a reign of terror begins to assert itself.

What can be done?

Firstly, the European governments, and the European political parties, must be compelled to put this question right at the centre of their agenda.

We may ask "can Europe afford to work?" This is the problem addressed by Allan Larsson, MP, speaking from Sweden. That question itself seems almost blasphemous. Is it not absurd that builders should be laid off, whilst the homeless huddle into cardboard boxes? How can we defend the dismissal of workers in the caring and social services, when distress has never been more visible?

Might not the biggest spender in any government's budget soon become the recuperation of the environment? If so, shouldn't this activity soon become a major employer? Judging by the comments we all heard during the Rio Summit, public opinion is quite ready to accept priorities of this kind; but will governments allocate the necessary resources to implement them?

Above all, a strategy to create jobs is now a matter for joint action between governments, as well as the European Community. This should have been the priority of the British Presidency of the Community, and the issue cannot be postponed much longer if disaster is to be avoided. Proposals along these lines form a large part of this book.

Meantime, there is one key area in which employees can exert an influence. This concerns the whole question of working time. The 40 hour week, with perhaps three weeks' holiday a year, and retirement at 60 or 65, represents patterns of work organization which were appropriate to the mechanical age, when economies were dominated by such industries as motors.

In the electronic age, such hours of work cannot be sustained. Not only do we need to agree much shorter stints of labour, but also much shorter working lifetimes. If the 21st century is not to become a hell, people need to weave in and out of educational courses throughout their lifetimes, in order to update their skills, and exploit their full human potential. At the same time, new technologies offer us the opportunity for immense improvements in the quality of family life. Maternity leave has become more and more significant, as it has become normal for women to stay at work while mothering young children. But now we can enter the age of paternity leave, as fathers are set free to help with child rearing, at the times when such help is most important.

Trade unions can help enormously by centring on questions such as the length of holidays, flexibility of retirement, and the shorter working week.

Today, this issue has become quite unavoidable. It is arguable that we shall never be able to sustain economic growth which would keep everybody in work in accordance with old rhythms. New technology will either force us to be free, by adopting more humane standards of working time, or it will set us apart into warring camps, haves against have-nots, employees against unemployed, each against all.

The 21st century could see a vast explosion of choice, which might really liberate everyone. Or it could be Yugoslavia, writ large, spreading mayhem everywhere.

CHAPTER 2

Can Europe Afford to Work?

Allan Larsson MP

Practically all European countries prefer to pay people to stay away from work, instead of preparing them for today's and tomorrow's demands. It is not lack of financial resources that force 16 to 17 million people into unemployment. The problem is a totally different one. That is why the question "can Europe afford to work?" has to be asked, and that is why we must go back to basics in our discussions about employment and economic development.

Allow me to develop my view of the European labour market, taking as a starting point an ongoing project within the Nordic social democratic parties. We discuss what contribution our Nordic countries and our parties can give to European development. To create a positive interest for Europe, we cannot confine the political discussion to institutions and treaties. We have to present to our fellow citizens a clear vision of a better Europe, and sound reforms that can solve Europe's fundamental problems.

We are concentrating our efforts in five main areas, where solutions must be sought at the European level:

— The first and fundamental area is employment. How will Europe be able to return to full employment?
— The second area is equality between men and women. How shall we organize our societies so that it will be possible for us to work on equal terms, and to have time and energy for our children?
— The third area is the environment. How can we save Europe's seas and lakes, beaches and rivers, clean water and clean air — the foundations of all life?
— The fourth area is the economy. How can we create a responsibility for the future, which includes long-term strengthening of public finances, as well as savings and investments?
— And the fifth area is Europe's global responsibility. How shall we create a secure Europe, not through walls, but through a new openness towards the new democracies in the east, and towards

the developing countries?

So, there are five "e's" on our agenda: employment, equality, environment, economy, and Europe's global responsibility.

Employment in Europe

What is the employment situation in Europe? In spite of strong and sustained economic growth, the eighties left behind unemployment which, in 1992, amounted to 16-17 million people in Western Europe, or 9 per cent of the workforce. Viewed internationally, the European picture is bleak. Unemployment is higher in Europe, compared to the United States or Japan. At the same time, the level of employment is lower in Europe than in the US and Japan. This means that unemployment is a heavier burden for Europe than appears to be the case when you only compare figures of relative unemployment. A major part of Europe's population has been excluded from the normal labour market. Many are long-term unemployed, totally dependent on benefits, and rejected by society.

Unemployment is also a heavy burden on public finances. In Western Europe (OECD Europe), the costs of unemployment benefits and early retirement can be calculated to be not less than 125 billion US dollars, or 100 billion ecus for 1992. On top of this comes the cost of extra compensations for unemployment, such as those based on collective agreements, amounting to huge sums.

The present situation involves enormous economic and social risks. There is a serious risk of high and permanent unemployment, with social conflicts and political extremism as a consequence.

When we look for explanations for this situation, we can see that Europe, during the eighties, has lagged behind international competition. This can clearly be seen when we compare Europe with Japan. During the eighties, Japan had an annual growth rate of 5 per cent; an inflation rate of 2.5 per cent; and an unemployment rate of 2.5 per cent. Japan has managed to combine low unemployment and low inflation, which has made possible rapid growth of economic resources.

During the same period, Western Europe had half that growth, twice that inflation, and three times the unemployment. When economic growth took off in Europe, the labour market did not react according to the dominating theories of the decade. People got stuck in long-term unemployment. In the Community alone, more than 6 million people are long term unemployed. This means that they have been without work for more than a year, which is an unreasonably long period. It would be more responsible to define six months without work as long-term unemployment.

When you have gone without work for so long, you lose touch with working life, and you lose faith in your own ability. You are no longer wanted by the labour market, and your existing skills are not an asset in a new job. Nor do you get access to those new skills which open doors to new opportunities. The way that labour market policies have been applied in Europe during the eighties looks like a demolition process. It gives the impression that the underlying theory is that Europe cannot afford to work.

At the same time, a series of studies has established that the shortage of skilled labour is a growing problem. This is due to the higher demand that is a consequence of a more knowledge intensive, more technically advanced, or more customer-geared production. In this way, the "mis-match" in the labour market worsened. There was no flexible adaption of supply and demand.

Through this rigidity, the European economy has become increasingly exposed to inflation. It is true that progress has been made in the fight against inflation, and that is very welcome. But, it is difficult to maintain stable prices when demand goes up. This, in turn, keeps interest rates up, and investment and growth down. The large residual unemployment is, thus, not an effective supply. We now experience the effects of this in the very high real interest rates in Europe, and the difficulties of getting a recovery.

It is important for Europe to get rid of inflation and the monetary instability that has hampered economic development. It is, however, not at all evident that monetary stability, which is the aim of the EMU, will automatically create jobs and welfare for all Europeans. There is a major risk that unemployment will remain high, and that social problems will grow, unless a clear strategy for sustained growth and full employment is established for the economic union.

What kind of labour market policy would make Europe perform better? Once again, there is good reason to compare Europe and Japan in order to highlight Europe's problems — but also its possibilities. Japan has no raw materials, and no energy resources. But it has one single asset that the country has used and developed in an extraordinary way. That is the productive qualities of its population.

When Japanese industry grows, there is a parallel development of the labour force. This takes the form of youth education and training, and higher education in universities and polytechnics; but, most of all, of adult training on the job. It is the many small improvements in daily work, and the learning process involved in this working method, which creates a large part of the dynamic of the Japanese economy. Through vigorous efforts in education, training, and improved skills, the Japanese are able to avoid bottlenecks, which fuel inflation, and redundancies, which cause unemployment.

Let us now look at Europe. When European industry develops, at a slower pace, both bottlenecks and redundancies occur. Education, training and skill development do not satisfy the needs of the individual, nor those of industry. Many countries in Europe are trapped in old-fashioned education systems, insufficient capacity for adult education and training, and outdated work organization.

A strong lever

We need a strong lever. That lesson is fundamental for the establishment of the Economic and Monetary Union, the EMU. The decision on EMU expresses the political power of financial Europe. The decision aims at a common currency, a common institution (the Central Bank), and a common timetable to reach the goal: a good discipline in the monetary field.

The agreement on the Social Dimension is much weaker. It lacks what creates the strength of EMU; namely, a clear, common goal, vigorous institutions, and a common timetable. There is a serious risk that the work to develop the real economy will lag behind monetary co-operation, which, in turn, will make it more difficult to establish monetary stability. If the Economic and Monetary Union is to become a reality, massive efforts need to be deployed in order to increase and equalize productivity in Europe.

The real lever for productivity and employment is to improve retraining, education and skill levels, and to reform work organization. We need more flexibility — not through a general lowering of workers' terms and conditions — but through higher skills and productivity for everyone. But, first of all, we need higher skills and productivity among those who are, or run the risk of becoming, unemployed.

Here a commitment is needed, and not only from the "social" powers of Europe. It is just as important that "monetary" Europe considers this to be a decisive point for the success of the EMU. They are the ones who should be the driving force in replacing the passive and unsuccessful labour market policies of the eighties with an active and developing policy. It is necessary to create a clear vision for the employment policy, which is just as clear and distinct as the one that applies to the monetary union policy today. This will be necessary if we are to turn Europe away from mass unemployment towards full employment.

A first clear vision of that kind should be to cut Europe's unemployment by half in the coming five years, and move 8 million unemployed Europeans from the dole towards active measures as a step to productive jobs in the ordinary labour market. Such a strategy does not mean that we need to increase public spending. What it will mean is a more rational use of our economic resources than we had during the eighties. This is evident when we look at the figures:

— with unemployment exceeding 16 million, or 9 per cent, in 1992;
— with public expenditure amounting to 125 billion dollars for unemployment or early retirement alone;
— with active measures amounting to less than half that sum, there are huge economic and social benefits to be gained from a new policy.

This strategy is about a changeover from social and income subsidies towards active measures to get the labour market to work, and to strengthen the whole economy. This way, unemployment can be changed into a positive supply, fertilizing the European economy. This is by far the most important structural policy measure for the nineties.

Such a change is, however, only one dimension of a new policy for full employment. The other dimension involves vigorous efforts to invest, both in industry and in infrastructure, such as the ETUC has drawn up in its statement on growth and employment strategy. With low inflation rates and an international economic upturn in the coming years, the scene is set for growth of private investment in Europe. Further, we need political decisions about public investment — especially in transport and energy — and responsible financing of these investments.

To implement such a strategy requires efforts covering a broad field. Efforts will be needed from business, from both sides of industry, from labour authorities and education systems, from national governments and parliaments, from the European Commission, from the Council of Ministers, and from the Parliament. New ideas and new initiatives are needed.

However, first and last, we need to rally around a new view of the European labour market, crossing national and interest boundaries. We must gather all good forces around a new constructive strategy to take care of Europe's possibilities. This must be based on the understanding that we can afford to work, and that it is only through our work that we can create the necesary resources for our private and social needs.

CHAPTER 3

The Dimensions of Recovery

Ken Coates MEP

The 1992 monetary crisis was generally reported as a threat to the process of European union. But, paradoxically, that same crisis offers the clearest possible support to the idea that a single European currency is a vital necessity.

Such a contradictory perspective cannot easily be translated into practical measures. How feasible is the transition to full European monetary union? The criteria of the Maastricht Treaty were elaborated in terms of monetary policy. They presumed existing levels of deregulation, and beneficial market conditions. Long before the Danish vote against the Treaty, recession had posed a large question-mark over the practicability of many of these criteria. Convergence between highly developed and less developed economies sounds all very well, if it reflects an improvement in the productive potential of the poorest. But one law for the lion and the ox is tyranny, and to impose tight limits on public indebtedness in richer and poorer countries alike would be to lock the poorest into dire recession.

Awareness of these problems stimulated the demand for a European Recovery Programme which would centre attention on full employment as the necessary bench-mark of progress towards integration. A modest commitment was made, after the Maastricht meeting, to the proposals known as the "Delors 2" package, allocating funds for the development of social cohesion in Spain, Portugal, Greece and Ireland. But even this package has not been honoured by the Council of Ministers, who are reluctant to apply the necessary resources to fulfil commitments which flow directly from the decisions of Maastricht. We shall return to this matter below.

After Black Wednesday

What lessons can be drawn from the great speculation of September 1992?

First of all, the sheer scale of that speculation gives us a picture of the ferocious monster which has been unleashed in the processes of deregulation. Today, more than ninety per cent of foreign exchange transactions concern currency speculation, as opposed to less than ten per cent during the age of exchange controls. That transnational companies become deeply embroiled in the game is no mitigation: on the contrary, it intensifies the casino atmosphere of the contemporary economy. Corporations play the currency markets, partly to avoid the punishment of prospective devaluation. But defensive speculation is a contradiction in terms, and the result of the September crash gives a fearful warning of things to come.

It must be said, in passing, that the manner of the British Government's departure from the Exchange Rate Mechanism was as damaging as any blow struck by the Major administration against European institutions. It created the maximum confusion and pressure on allied states. Britain delayed seeking realignment until it was already too late, and then arbitrarily devalued by unilaterally breaking from the agreement. The result was further mayhem, much of which might have been avoided if there had been a serious attempt to reach agreement about the realignment of currencies within the mechanism.

We have now reached the point in which the case for a single currency is *social and economic* more than it is financial. Which country on its own can afford increased expenditure on job creation, or on social allocations, when its currency is vulnerable to the slightest movement in the foreign exchanges? It is not necessary to envisage a conspiracy to enforce Thatcherite programmes on reluctant governments. The speculative army, following the instincts of the wolf pack, will achieve conformity, all unbidden. If the invisible hand is supposed to regulate this process, its enforcement will be all too visible, red in tooth and claw. If governments are ever to recover the capacity to plan for higher levels of investment and expenditure, they will need to work together while moving towards the strength of the single currency. They may well also need to restrict the power of speculation by devising an appropriately progressive common tax on currency transactions, refundable only on the basis of hard evidence of their economic and social justification. Such a tax would penalise speculators and it would not be difficult to introduce alongside the Exchange Rate Mechanism. It could be maintained for external transactions after the advent of monetary union. Some estimates maintain that even an initial standard tax of a quarter of one per cent on such transactions would inhibit speculation by rendering it quite unprofitable for a large part of the time. Higher rates could be imposed on very large deals, or during periods of intense pressure. Of course, no individual government could control such transactions, but if all were to act together a tax would be perfectly feasible.

Public needs, not private gain

All this implies a resumption of the priority of public needs over private gain in the determination of exchange rate realignments. Evidently, Maastricht alone is not enough to produce such an outcome. Moreover, monetary union in the Maastricht style, as we have already seen, assumes measures which are highly deflationary. Strong though the measures for the single market may prove, countries balanced on the knife-edge between recession and depression will find a limit of three per cent of GDP on budget deficits, as required for monetary union, far too restrictive. Of course, temporary derogations are permitted by the Maastricht Treaty. But in some countries, temporary relief is not likely to be sufficient. It is one thing to pursue policies which ensure that overall Community expenditure is not inflationary. But the unevenness of economic development within the Community insists on flexibility in pursuit of this policy. Where ten, fifteen or twenty per cent of the workforce is unemployed, public expenditure need not be inflationary. Work done by Stuart Holland and a team of economists reveals that the unemployment trends in the Community are most forbidding. Given the present low expectations of growth, and assuming weak cohesion, it is likely that the average unemployment rate in the Community could be as high as twelve or twelve and a half per cent by the turn of the century. Some analysts put it higher, at up to fifteen. This would give national and regional figures which are quite incompatible with the maintenance of present social institutions in some countries. On the worst guesses, almost twenty-five per cent of the Spanish population could lack work. Thirteen per cent could be unemployed in France. In Germany, even, the figure would rise to nine per cent, with youth unemployment at approximately twice the rate of general unemployment. Small wonder that areas of despair for youth correlate with the rise of racism and extremism.

The Stuart Holland team, which continues the ten-year old labours that were begun in the project, *Out of Crisis*, has produced detailed calculations based on an estimation of the effects of different variables on the likely unemployment levels in all the countries of the present European Community by 2000 AD (see Table 1).

Table 1:
Unemployment in Europe, 2000 AD

Country	If cohesion expenditure is minimal		If cohesion expenditure is strong		If strong cohesion is linked to strong growth and 5% reduced working time
	1.5% growth rate	*3.5% growth rate*	*1.5% growth rate*	*3.5% growth rate*	
European Community	14.2%	10.6%	13.6%	10.0%	8.3%
Belgium	14.9%	11.8%	14.8%	11.7%	9.9%
Denmark	9.3%	6.4%	9.1%	6.3%	4.2%
Germany	9.5%	5.9%	9.4%	5.8%	5.8%
Greece	11.6%	9.2%	9.3%	7.0%	4.9%
Spain	24.4%	19.1%	22.1%	16.8%	14.7%
France	16.1%	13.0%	15.8%	12.8%	10.7%
Ireland	25.6%	22.6%	23.2%	20.2%	18.2%
Italy	15.6%	11.8%	14.3%	10.6%	8.5%
Luxembourg	4.4%	0.9%	4.3%	0.8%	0.8%
Netherlands	13.1%	9.2%	12.9%	9.1%	7.5%
Portugal	9.0%	4.8%	8.1%	4.0%	2.1%
United Kingdom	12.3%	9.3%	12.3%	9.2%	7.0%
East Germany	9.7%	7.1%	9.4%	6.8%	
East + West Germany	9.6%	6.2%	9.4%	6.0%	

The variables involve high and low growth rates, and strong and weak cohesion programmes. By way of assumption, estimates are made on the outcome of growth rates of 1.5 per cent and 3.5 per cent respectively. These are combined with projections of the results of maintaining present "low" levels of cohesion expenditure, and the outcome of "strong" social policies, which involve an increase of the Community budget of 0.44 per cent of European GDP by 1997, rising to 0.60 per cent by 2002, a large part of which would fund external and internal cohesion programmes. As the table shows, strong cohesion plus high growth could diminish unemployment by one-third in the Community as a whole. A similar reduction would pertain in Germany and Spain. Britain, France and Ireland would achieve a twenty-five per cent reduction. The overall average would then be ten per cent. Even better results could be achieved by average reductions of five per cent in working time, which are necessary because the productivity obtained with new technologies constantly outstrips the enlargement of market demand.

Shorter working time

Whilst it is clear that shorter working time involves today, as it always has, keen bargaining in industry, and the likelihood of sharp contests, trade unions are likely to see the struggle for reduced hours as a key strategy for job creation and control over the allocation of working time. Already the 1500-hour year is within reach in Germany and bolder ideas are gaining currency. The sharing of child-minding and domestic commitments adds to the pressure for cuts in working time and the recognition of new rights to domestic leave. The training revolution which new technology demands reinforces the need for paid educational leave, and indeed for educational access throughout working life. We should expect the European Parliament to endorse this case, and recommend it as a priority item for the social dialogue between employers and unions in Europe (involving UNICE and the ETUC). This is necessary because no solid progress can be made piecemeal by one country at a time, since those who refuse will receive a competitive advantage in the short term even if they lose out in the end.

But necessary though it is, this argument is not enough. Evidently it must be conjoined to political and economic action at every level, from locality, to nation, to Community.

What precedents are there for a European Recovery Programme? They are quite clear.

The Japanese example

The Japanese announced a special recovery programme, in the summer of 1992, involving a total expenditure of 61.4 billion ecu (£43b). And the Japanese have been adding supplementary packages since then. The Japanese programme is almost the same as the total Community annual budget, of 63.2 billion ecu. It is comprehensively vast, and calculated to prime pumps in every sector of economic activity. Yen expenditure equivalent to 27.1 billion ecus is to be allocated to public works and infrastructure. Of that sum, the yen equivalent of 7.1 billion ecus will be allocated for regional and local programmes. If replicated in the Community, a programme of this magnitude would take EC structural funds to 24.8 billion ecus, a level they would not reach until some years into the twenty-first century on current projections. No less than the equivalent of 28.5 billion ecus are to be injected by Japan into the financial system: not only to fortify weakened banks, but to boost development through special low-interest loans.

Can Europe afford to do less than Japan for its economic recovery? And how should this recovery be organized? It is no longer possible for nation states to be the motors of recovery. The main engine must surely be the emerging Community. These are contentious questions, but we do not have long to answer them.

Speaking to the Socialist Group in the European Parliament, Jacques Delors said in 1992:

> We must bear in mind one figure. In 1997, Community expenditure will represent only 3 per cent of the total public expenditure of the member states. I myself had calculated the necessary amount at 5 per cent in the framework of economic and monetary union, and in the framework of subsidiarity, properly applied . . .

In point of fact, the Delors 2 package, as it has become known, was halved at Edinburgh and has been the object of a continued filibuster, in spite of the fact that it has been a rather modest project. True, it has been misrepresented by various national governments, some of whom have complained that it proposed a 30 per cent increase in Community expenditure. In fact, the increase which is projected would amount to 15 per cent, devoted to economic and social cohesion expenditure. This would be matched by national expenditure of an equivalent amount. But the national expenditure would come from the recipient state, and not be levied across the Community as a whole. Be that as it may, nobody could possibly compare this programme with the Japanese recovery effort, and think that it might substitute for a matching European Recovery Programme.

Here, we must face another paradox. Under the Maastricht Treaty, there is to be a restrictive three per cent of GDP limit on government deficits, which has already fuelled strong criticism in the debate on the ratification of the Treaty. Such a limit would certainly inhibit national decisions on recovery expenditure. Actions short of full-scale community involvement will be divisive, and will in any case prove unlikely to succeed. Only a major increase in the Community's own budget would facilitate the development of a recovery programme on anything like an appropriate scale.

Social expenditure

To this dilemma, we must join the urgent question of the deflation of social expenditure, which accompanies every recession, and will prove exceptionally marked in the present deep depression which has hit some countries. Social expenditure needs to be deflation-proofed.

Here, we encounter the major weakness in the Maastricht framework, which is most sharply reflected in the decision to allow the British Government to opt out of the entire Social Chapter. But that Social Chapter is by no means as strong as it should be, and it leaves much to be desired in the area of social cohesion. The Delors 2 package shows a distinct awareness of this problem, and insists that competitiveness and cohesion should be the two main dimensions of Community action in the 1990s. It also suggests an extension of cohesion funds into additional areas.

Not all social cohesion policies involve major expenditure. Both at the national and Community level, there are many policies of direct interest to working people which do not weigh heavily on the budgets. Let us list some of these which should be carried out in unison:

(1) Reduced working hours would impose costs on employers to the extent that they were not matched by productivity increases. But the structural problem of modern industry is that productivity increases far outrun potential market growth. A five per cent reduction in working time throughout the Community would almost halve the volume of unemployment to be anticipated by the year 2000. In optimum conditions, unemployment would come down to slightly over eight per cent in the whole area of the Community, without entailing any significant budgetary change.

(2) Likewise, the establishment of rights for women and other employees can be widely secured without involving substantial spending. The right to negotiate flexible working hours to suit family needs can, with modern technologies, improve productivity at no additional cost.

(3) Industrial innovation should have been underpinned by the pluri-annual research and development programmes in the Maastricht draft text, to which the British Government took exception. These proposals were both necessary and timely, and should be revived. The key is the combination of some Community expenditure with a vast innovative effort by leading firms.

(4) Europe will not meet the challenge of Japanese competition if it does not transform the status of labour on the shopfloor, enabling greatly closer co-operation. This implies joint action rather than expenditure. We need an active Community to sponsor new innovation agreements in key sectors, and a participatory style of management. These elements of the Social Charter and the social dialogue could bring immense improvements to productivity, at minimal cost.

(5) The enhancement of the scope for small and middle sized enterprises through networking in production, marketing, and innovation will enlarge the possibility of improvement for both manufacturing and sales. This can develop through the Community's RECITE and OUVERTURE programmes, which should be augmented and matched by other specialized initiatives. The

promotion of networking by the Community can ensure that relatively small seed corn expenditures produce considerable returns which generate great gains both for the participating companies, and the nation states within which they are operating. This is a key dimension of regional policy, to which Community regions themselves could commit resources. It needs systematic encouragement and expansion, not least by the new Committee of the Regions.

Global recovery

None of these measures is entirely without cost if carried out collectively, but all can produce immediate and tangible benefits. However, the key question must remain one of substantial funding for a recovery programme, which can match the initiative taken in Japan, and thus help to ensure that the world economy does not slide through recession into deep depression and slump. Unless Europe is prepared to will such a programme, there will be no conceivable means of addressing the global problems which have already suffocated trade in many developing nations. It is possible that the political agenda may be eased by the result of the American elections. But European response cannot simply wait on such beneficial changes, which may not happen. Europe's role in the world is sufficiently powerful to demand that we take our responsibilities for fostering global recovery, not only by international assistance, but also by reform of the conditions in which it operates.

The expansion of exports is absolutely inhibited by a wall of debt. Many underdeveloped countries are steadily sliding back, rather than advancing, in the grip of this debt. The collapse of primary commodity prices follows directly on the pattern which we have seen before, in the 1930s, and before that in the 1880s. In the 1880s, the fall in commodity prices relative to the prices of manufactured goods was round about twenty-five per cent. In the thirties, this fall accelerated to fifty per cent, broadly the same as today's. The resultant pattern of default created the Baring brothers scandal in the eighties, when London's leading Merchant House had to be bailed out by the Bank of England with Government support. Government support was inadequate to prevent many of the failures of the 1930s, in spite of the creation of innumerable financial buttresses to shore up debt repayment. Michael Barratt Brown has documented this dreadful story, in a paper on commodity prices and debt, which offers a fearful warning to us today, at the present turn in global fortunes.

All these problems are likely to be aggravated by the failure of the GATT talks, unless a miracle intervenes. Positive steps to write off debt and correct widening inequalities are needed, if purchasing power is to be re-established worldwide. No single government can do this without risking isolation and competitive strangulation. But if the European Community took the lead in an expansion programme, it could generate great pressures on the USA and Japan to follow behind. Instead, we seem to be poised on a new escalation of trade wars, with incalculable consequences. Were substantial resources focused on the developing countries, European exports would rise in concert with the recovery of such countries. But if the debt and misery are to be reinforced, then they will suck in to their vortex many of those who have felt themselves to be immune from disaster.

A recovery budget

Stuart Holland and Francis Cripps have offered a series of alternative projections of the European Community budget, between 1992 and 2012 (see Table 2).

Table 2:
Projections of the Community Budget for alternative expansion programmes (billion 1992 ECU)

	1992	1997	2002	2012
BASE PROJECTION				
Structural Funds	17.7	20.2	22.9	29.4
External action	3.4	3.9	4.4	5.6
Other policies	42.1	48.1	54.5	69.9
Total	63.2	72.2	81.9	105.0
(per cent of GNP)	(1.15)	(1.15)	(1.15)	(1.15)
LOW PROJECTION				
Structural Funds	17.7	28.6	50.0	80.0
External action	3.4	6.1	11.6	21.3
Other policies	42.1	50.6	61.6	84.8
Total	63.2	85.2	123.2	186.2
(per cent of GNP)	(1.15)	(1.34)	(1.59)	(1.75)
HIGH PROJECTION				
Structural funds	17.7	44.3	62.9	88.3
External action	3.4	10.3	16.8	29.4
Other policies	42.1	54.6	66.7	93.6
Total	63.2	109.2	146.3	211.2
(per cent of GNP)	(1.15)	(1.59)	(1.75)	(1.80)

The table estimates the size of Community budgets, allowing for economic growth, assuming first the continuation of present policies, secondly a "low cohesion" scenario, and thirdly, assuming a "high cohesion" scenario. These figures reflect the possibilities for external assistance, and for increases in structural funding.

> "In the low and high cohesion scenarios, we have assumed that spending on 'external action' will rise from ECU 3.4 billion in 1992 to twenty to thirty billion in 2012, while the budget for structural funds will rise from ECU 17.7 billion (1992) to eighty to ninety billion (2012)."

These calculations are based on a series of assumptions of growth rates which are tabulated in Table 3.

Table 3:
Budget as a Percentage of Community GNP

	Now	*1997*	*2002*	*2012*
Base	1.15	1.15	1.15	1.15
Low cohesion		+0.19	+0.44	+0.60
		1.34	1.59	1.75
High cohesion		+0.44	+0.60	+0.65
		1.59	1.75	1.80

The base projection presumes that the budget will remain constant as a percentage of Community GNP, at 1.15. Of course, the size of the budget would still increase as a result of growth in the gross national product, and enlargement of Community membership.

The low cohesion scenario would increase the budget by 0.19 per cent in 1997 to 0.44 in 2002, to 0.60 in 2012, mainly from expansion of the Commission to include former EFTA members. The high cohesion budget would augment these increases substantally, to 0.44 in 1997, and 0.65 in 2012.

It is on these calculations that the projections of potential employment recorded above in Table I, and the substantial discussion, have been founded.

Dismal though the present outlook appears, after the collapse of sterling, these estimates should show us that there is a way forward, out of crisis. That way depends upon joint action. In the circumstances of the 1990s such joint action should naturally be led by the Commission, and co-ordinated with member governments. Not only will this be easier than the arrangement of convergent national initiatives outside the framework of the European

Community, but it will provide a necessary catalyst to cross-border flows which can be calculated to maximize development possibilities, and the multiplier effect which these can exert. Of course the more thorough the attendant convergence of incomes and social cohesion can be, the more dynamic the recovery will prove. But this will require completely different policies from the restrictions on public expenditure which obsess so many Governments in Europe, and above all from the dogmas which still dominate the reflexes of Government in Britain.

CHAPTER 4

Money, Debt and Slump

Michael Barratt Brown

I
What Money?

After the debacle of "black September" 1992, Mr Major committed his government amid much patriotic flag wagging to preserve the pound sterling, even if it is to be worth less than it was. Of course, every nation wants to have its own money; and it is not just as a totem of national virility that nations want their own symbol on their own currency — a king or queen's head or founding president. Having your own money gives certain real power to a national government. That is one of the chief reasons why nations want to be states; then, not only can they raise taxes and borrow money against state assets, but they can print money to pay their soldiers and civil servants and generate other employment. Without that power local government, whatever other constitutional rights it has, is financially dependent on the nation state. So, we have now something over 300 separate states in the world today. Unions and federations are breaking up, and for many of the new states, like Croatia or Lithuania, it is a major aim to have their own money, at the very least to get out from under the burden of foreign debts of a disintegrating Yugoslavia or Soviet Union, debts which they blame on their one-time dominant partners, Serbia and Russia.

There are fifty-five states in Africa alone, all with their own money, and almost all heavily in debt to foreign bankers who lent them money, and particularly to the International Monetary Fund and the World Bank. In their desperate bid for dollars they compete with each other in the markets for their primary commodities, and as a result the prices of these commodities go steadily down and they can buy less and less of the manufactured goods they need from outside. And that means trade declines all round. This is how it was in the 1930s; and, when the IMF and the World Bank were set up at Bretton Woods in 1944, it was the intention that their management of international finance would mean that each state did not have to compete like this for a share of a declining market. Such hopes have been sorely dashed, so that today nation after nation looks to its own state to manage its own money.

Can nation states today manage their own money?

Twelve of the nation states of Europe are nonetheless considering whether and how they might give up their sovereign power to have their own money. How can this be possible that they should be embarking upon some kind of federal arrangements when other federations are collapsing all around them? In looking at the debtor countries of Africa, we saw that they all wanted dollars. Some money is worth more than others, so that some currencies are called "soft" — they are good only for trade inside their country of origin — and some are called "hard" — they can be used in international trade. Any state can have its own money and it will be accepted as currency within its borders, but if its citizens want to trade outside their money may not be accepted. Whether it is will depend on what it will buy ouside or inside. Some states could opt for autarky and simply cut themselves off from outside trade. Many are too small to do this, and in a world that is increasingly interlocked by transport and communication systems and by multiple sourcing of production, it becomes ever more difficult, as well as politically unacceptable, for any state, however large, to adopt a policy of complete isolation.

What, then, makes a currency hard or soft? Is this something that each state can ensure for itself? In 1992 we saw that even a very large and powerful state like the United Kingdom could not keep up the value of its currency, when others thought it was overvalued. Why was this so? Why did foreigners, and British traders also for that matter, not want British pounds at that value, so that the speculators knew that they could sell pounds today at a high price and be certain to buy them back tomorrow at a lower price? The answer is that foreigners did not want to buy British goods and services as much as British people wanted to buy foreign goods and services. There was in effect a massive deficit in the balance of payments between the UK and the rest of the world. British goods were simply not competitive at the existing exchange rate. The country was living on borrowed money, and the only way to continue that kind of living was to offer higher interest rates to anyone who held pounds than those offered on other currency holdings. But those were then the interest rates paid by British industry when British firms borrowed money, and that of course made most of British industry's costs higher and its products even less competitive.

In these circumstances, it is, therefore, argued by some that all this shows that British money should not be tied to anyone else's money — in the European Exchange Rate Mechanism (the ERM), let alone in some tighter European Monetary Union. But, it wasn't the ERM that fixed the exchange rate; there could have been a realignment within the system. The Italian government let that cat out of the bag. It was the government that fixed the rate and tried to keep it up, spending many billions of reserves and of borrowed money to do so. That may have been very stupid, the government was certainly ill-advised, but the important point is that it wasn't feasible. All the much vaunted national sovereignty — to have your own money, so that the government could keep up its value — came in the end to nothing.

Now, this vulnerability of a national currency to outside pressure puts very strict limits on what governments can do on their own. The goods and services produced inside their state have to be competitive with those from outside, and that means especially that the rate of inflation inside must not be above the average outside. A single state that went on a spending spree and reduced its interest rate to create employment, and as a result created inflation as demand soared and increased the foreign payments deficit, would soon be brought to heel. There would not even be a delay in today's world while the effects of such a policy worked themselves out; deposits in the currency of that state would be removed the moment the policy was announced. The value of the currency in relation to others would collapse, the cost of imports would rise and access to international credit would be put in jeopardy. The government would be powerless to prevent this, because the greater part of the world's trade in goods and services today takes place inside giant transnational companies which move their funds from place to place, paying bills here and delaying payment elsewhere, according to their estimate of the relative future movements in exchange rates.

Why not an international monetary union?

It would seem to be obvious from the foregoing analysis that the only way for governments of nation states to create employment, and to get out of a general economic recession like the present one, would be for all to agree to act together. Mr Major's government and some other governments believe that they can make their countries' goods competitive by devaluing their currencies, and keep down the inflation that might follow from higher import prices by cutting back on public spending. But if other governments also do the same, you get a competitive devaluation and deepening recession as each state digs a deeper and deeper hole in its spending power. This is what happened in the 1930s, and the result was that recession led to world-wide slump, and slump to fascism and war. The exact opposite course would appear to be the right one for governments to agree for all to adopt together. Spending power could be everywhere increased up to the capacity of productive resources to meet it. Beyond that, inflation would get out of hand — and it would be important to recognize that limitation. There would also be problems with regions whose productive capacity and productivity were inadequate, and these would have to be assisted from the more productive regions. This is what West Germans are doing for the East, and it involves a rather unpopular check to growth of the standard of living in the West. The same principle could be applied more widely, not only in Europe, but also between the industrialized nations and those in course of development. The result would be continuous world-wide expansion in living stan-dards, instead of gathering recession developing into slump. The nature of the expansion would need to be related to environmental limitations, but these need not be prohibitive of all development. So, why is it not done? Why, instead, do we have the spectacle of states playing beggar-my-neigbour, with even the biggest and most powerful in trouble, and the little ones facing disaster?

What, then, is wrong with international monetary agreements? It may be rewarding to look at what happened last time that there was a major world economic recession — in the slump of the 1930s. A World Economic Conference was called in 1933 and held in the Geological Museum in London, presided over by Ramsay MacDonald. It failed to agree to end any of the beggar-my-neighbour devices, which all the delegates said they deplored. The United States government began a competitive devaluation of its currency. Germany, Italy, and Japan reneged on their debts, and set out to build militarized states and embark on imperial expansion — the "Have-nots" against the "Haves". Expenditure on rearmament everywhere gave the world economy the stimulus it needed. There was a brief check in 1937. Crops of coffee and grain continued to be burned to bring supply and demand more nearly into line at a price that kept the growers alive. But it was the approach of war, and then the war itself, that provided demand enough to establish the full employment of human and other resources. Nobody wants or wanted that again. So, what was to be done when the war ended? It was unthinkable that there should be a return to the beggar-my-neighbour years of the 1930s. Wartime promises had been made to end all that, enshrined in Britain's Beveridge plan, and in President Roosevelt's New Deal.

II
Slump: Last Time and This Time

By 1943, it seemed possible in the Allied camp to begin to believe that the war could be won, and statesmen's eyes turned to post-war reconstruction. In Britain, John Maynard Keynes, as an unpaid Treasury adviser, came increasingly to be accepted as the leading authority on post-war international monetary policy. It was crucially important that it should have been Keynes. He had made a name for himself not only by the effectiveness of his exposition of the policy of spending your way out of a slump, but also by his earlier ridiculing of the policy of demanding reparations from Germany after the First World War. The result, he pointed out, was to undermine the market in Germany for the Allies' exports. The same argument applied to the British demand for the repayment of debt by Argentina and the Eastern European countries when the prices of their primary commodity exports collapsed. (It applies equally to the requirement of debt repayment from Third World countries today.) Keynes saw the absence of effective demand due to unequal economic development as the main cause of the deep and prolonged slump of the 1930s. The answer was to boost demand by easy money policies combined with redistribution from the rich to the poor, applied universally, so that all were equally affected and none could escape into competitive beggar-my-neighbour practices.

The Keynes Plan, as it developed in negotiation with the Americans, was a bold attempt to create a multilateral world-wide monetary and trading system to replace unilateral nation state sovereignty over exchange rates and trade protection. Building a new international economic order required not only strong international institutions for the long term, but financial support for the reconstruction of war-torn Europe in the short term. Harry Dexter White of the US Treasury also had a Plan — the White Plan — for an International Fund for short-term lending to be based on a limited pooling of the gold holdings of the several member states, and an International Bank that would offer to underwrite long-term loans in the world's money markets.

The Keynes Plan had three institutional elements to support an international money — an international clearing union (providing overdrafts like a High Street bank), and a stabilization fund to meet the short-term deficits of member states from funds provided by creditor members (this had to be reconciled with Harry White's International Monetary Fund); an international bank for reconstruction with its own funds to provide for longer term structural problems (this had to be reconciled with White's International Bank for Reconstruction and Development based on the money markets, which came to be generally known as the World Bank); and an international trade organization to encourage and regulate commercial collaboration (this, the International Trade Organization [ITO], was not part of the White Plan and was to emerge much modified as GATT, the General Agreement on Tariffs and Trade). Keynes believed that, with his institutions in place and adequately financed by the creditor nations through a pooling of their reserves, it would be possible to fix exchange rates over a considerable period of time. As with the European Exchange Rate Mechanism today, there would be the opportunity for agreed realignment if this became evidently necessary, but in the meantime stability would be achieved and competitive devaluation outlawed. The institutions in the White Plan looked rather the same as those proposed by Keynes, but the Bank had only the funds available in existing money markets to deploy, and the input to the Fund from pooling the reserves of both the debtor and the creditor nations, especially the USA, was very limited. Quotas were to be set for each country's contribution of its own currency, and this would set the limit of the foreign currency that it could call upon. Of course, the debtor countries wanted the quotas set high, and the creditors insisted on setting them low. The Soviet Union was particularly angry at the size of the quota that White had set for it ($1 billion), and in the event pulled out of the whole Bretton Woods system, regarding the conditions to be attached to drawing rights as a brazen act of United States imperialism.

The Keynes Plan

The Keynes Plan was, thus, really very different from the White Plan. It depended on certain assumptions that Keynes made explicit: first, that states in deficit could draw enough funds from the clearing union and stabilization fund automatically so as to stop them taking alternative protectionist measures. Secondly, that the bank would have adequate funds of its own to make available for repairing war-time destruction and ensuring rapid economic recovery. Thirdly, that the trade organization would provide for action to reduce tariffs, preferences, and other protectionist devices while maintaining the commitment to what was termed "approximately full employment". Fourthly, that the Fund and the Bank would be truly international, credits and debits being expressed in the books in international units of account, this money to be called "Bancor".

And, finally, that, in Keynes's own words, "the officials of the two bodies would, in the course of time, come to regard themselves as primarily international officials, taking a world, objective outlook, and only where clearly necessary grinding their own national axes."

The world in which Keynes had lived and worked was one where there was no dominant world power, as Britain had been in the Nineteenth Century. This fact was reflected in the provision for permanent members of the Security Council of the United Nations, each with an equal right to a veto — the USA, UK, France, the Soviet Union and China — to which no doubt in due course Germany and Japan would be added. In 1944, as the war drew to an end, however, it transpired that there was only one power which had any money left — the USA. The others had spent every last penny on buying arms and other supplies from the United States, before the US entered the war and made arms and other supplies available on lend-lease. Keynes's clearing union and international bank were to be formed by a pooling of nation states' reserves, but these would have to come almost entirely from the United States, and the sums Keynes wanted were very large indeed — overdraft facilities of $26 billions for the clearing union with $5 billion in the stabilization fund, and a capital fund of $10 billion for the Bank. Some 85% of these totals would have to be contributed from the US. (Multiply by 15 to arrive at equivalent figures in today's money.) At the same time, the United States would be expected to forgo lend-lease debts and start to reduce its tariffs and other protectionist measures under the ITO, without, as it seemed to Congressional opponents of these proposals, getting in advance any reduction in British sterling controls and imperial preferences.

There was no chance that the United States would agree to hand over such sums or such powers to international civil servants to provide what Congress regarded as "spendthrift" governments almost unlimited resources to play with. Senator Taft spoke of "pouring good American money down a rat hole". There was some particularly straight speaking in Congress about British imperial designs that the United States was being asked to finance. As most leading Americans saw it, the US dollar was henceforth to replace the pound sterling, and there was to be no truck with any other international currency — whatever it was called, certainly not something called "bancor", to take the place of gold. By the end of the war, nearly the whole of the world's gold reserves had been accumulated in Fort Knox. It was inevitable that US policy makers should think of returning to the gold standard. The original requirement of the White Plan had been that subscriptions to the Fund should be in gold, and exchange rates fixed in terms of gold.

Keynes had succeeded in arguing White out of this requirement on the grounds that it would be excessively restrictionist, in effect to restrict the expansion of world trade to the rate of growth of the world's gold supply. It was just this that Keynes wished to get away from, having seen the disastrous results of Britain's return, in 1925, to linking sterling to gold (the gold standard). But he also hoped to establish a world money that was not any one country's money, and thus subject to that country's trade balance at the time.

In the event, Keynes had to abandon his more expansionist concepts of overdraft facilities in his clearing union, and his hopes of establishing an international money issued by an international bank. In the agreement that was finally reached, in July 1944, at Bretton Woods, New Hampshire, a Fund and a Bank were established, but very much under United States control (as we shall see), and with much smaller resources than Keynes had hoped for. What the United States in the end put into the Fund was $3.175 billion towards total resources of $8.8 billion. The Bank was allowed to raise capital up to $10 billion, but for many years little of this was issued. There were to be no "free meals". Funds were to be made available, but on strict conditions.

The needs of Europe were not, however, neglected. The US government found another way of supporting reconstruction, which kept its support under firm US control and limited it to friendly states. This was the Marshall Plan, which assisted post-war recovery in Japan and in Western Europe including Germany. The sums involved were not much less than Keynes had proposed, some $17 billions in Western Europe alone, spread over a four year period. In addition, we should take into account the settlement of the UK's Lend-Lease obligations of $20 billion, and an Anglo-American loan of some $3 billions. The UK squandered most of the money on an abortive attempt to keep the Sterling Area afloat as a rival to the dollar area. The rest of Western Europe and Japan made remarkable recoveries using the aid for major public works to restore the shattered infrastructure of their economies and launch their respective "economic miracles". No similar aid was made available for the Soviet Bloc, or the undeveloped countries of the Third World, and it was many years before the IMF and the World Bank turned their attention in these directions.

The lessons

What is important for our problems today is the way in which control of an international monetary union was perceived, and, in the end, realized at Bretton Woods. It is wrong to think of the

Anglo-American argument as being primarily between the defenders of a dying British Empire and the antagonists of an emergent United States world hegemony. It was much more an argument about international or national management of the world's money. Multilateralism against protectionism was how this choice was seen, but the argument was itself cut across by conservative and radical views on the role of government in managing the economy. Harry White was a committed multilateralist, for whom Keynes had been a guru in his years as a university economics professor before his meteoric rise through the US Treasury. White and his Secretary of the Treasury, Morgenthau, were also expansionists, who believed in strong government driving what Morgenthau called the "usurious money lenders from the temple of international finance". Ten years later, a US Attorney General was to charge White with being a communist spy. A great body of Congressional opinion, chiefly in the Republican ranks, was both protectionist and anti-government (however self-contradictory that may seem), as well as being quite violently anti-British. They were only able to unite around policies that were manifestly pro-American and anti-Soviet. When it came to looking at the Bretton Woods institutions, these were seen quite frankly as instruments of US foreign policy. The IMF and World Bank were to be situated in Washington, the Governor of the Bank would be an American, as would 40% of the executive directors, and most of the top officials. To ensure further that the US had the dominant voice, the executive directors were to be full-time officials subordinated to an Advisory Council on International Monetary and Financial Problems, which would itself be a US cabinet committee chaired by the Secretary of the Treasury.

So much for Keynes's hopes that the officials of the Fund and the Bank would "come to regard themselves as primarily international officials . . . not grinding their own national axes". Far from this happening, US domination of the Fund and the Bank has continued, although the relative strength of the US in the world economy has been mortally challenged by both Japan and Germany. Even the Advisory Council to the Governor provided for in the Bank's Articles of Association, to be selected with as wide an international representation as possible, has never been activated; nor has the provision on each loan committee of the Bank for a "representative of the member (state) in whose territory a project is located". The Bretton Woods institutions — the World Bank and more particularly the IMF — have come to be seen by recipients of their funding as so eminently interventionist and conservative in their requirements that it is hard to remember that they were once seen by Keynes, even in the much modified form which was finally adopted, as in any way instruments of international expansionary policies.

Expansion

The fact is that there were deep divisions over the Bretton Woods agreements in the British camp as well as in the United States. Keynes had only very qualified support from Sir Kingsley Wood, the Chancellor of the Exchequer in Churchill's War Cabinet up to his death at the end of 1943. Kingsley Wood regarded all expansionist policies with deep suspicion, above all the proposals in the Beveridge report with its apparently unlimited commitment of future tax payers money to some "New Jerusalem" in Britain after the war. His support for Bretton Woods as "an orderly and agreed method of determining the value of national currency units, to eliminate unilateral action . . ." and make governments "subject to the check of consultations with the other governments", was tempered by the conclusion that this would depend on the belief that governments "would conduct their affairs with prudence . . ."

Those in Britain who most favoured an expansionist policy came from the Left and the Right. They were not only strongly opposed to any return to the gold standard but opposed all forms of multilateralism, believing, as their successors still do today, that only the freedom of a nation state to manage its own money can allow it to create the conditions for full employment and social advance. Sir Robert Boothby, a staunch Conservative defender of the Sterling Area who dubbed the American loan an "economic Munich", told the House of Commons that "the White Plan will be the end . . . the end of all our hopes of an expansionist policy . . . the end of the Beveridge Plan . . . the end of the new Britain we are fighting to rebuild. It will lead again to world depression, to chaos and ultimately to war." The Beaverbrook Press thundered against any attempt to put the "American Treasury in the position of having a veto over decisions to change the value of sterling". For American Treasury read the German central bankers and we know where we are.

Keynes, in presenting his plan both to the Churchill Government and to a wider public, had to steer a difficult course between emphasizing the freedom that remained to national governments, which were likely to be in debt to the Fund and Clearing Union (the British government included), to pursue policies of expansion, and the requirement of creditors (particularly of the United States) that some conditions should be imposed on continuous overdrawing by the debtors without adequate corrective policies. Keynes feared above all deflationary policies in the creditor countries leading to widespread unemployment. His opponents in Britain and America feared above all inflationary policies in the debtor countries leading to general monetary collapse. The compromise, as we have seen, was to eliminate the overdraft provision of Keynes's clearing union, and to provide for a quite small automatic access to the first tranche of the Fund, further tranches being made subject to successively more stringent imposed conditions — conditions that are known only too well to debtor countries today. Since 1944 the restrictionist philosophy built into the Fund has been reinforced. Inflation (inspite of all the restrictions) has eaten into the value of the first tranches, and the value of Fund and Bank resources has never kept up with the growth in the value of world trade.

The judgement of history must be that for more than thirty years the Bretton Woods institutions presided over the most rapid expansion in world trade and development that had ever been seen. But were they in any way responsible? The answer must be — not entirely. There were other — partly technological — causes of the latest long cycle in capitalist world economic activity, but one of the causes must be said to confirm Keynes's view of the need for income redistribution to generate expansion. This was the steady outflow of gold from the United States due to the persistence of deficits in the United States balance of foreign payments. In effect, the United States was buying more than it sold in trade with the rest of the world, and paying first with gold from Fort Knox and then, when that was run down to a strategic minimum, with Euro-dollars.

For a long time, the rest of the world was happy to increase its gold and dollar reserves and calculate its foreign payments in dollars, but in the end doubts began to be raised about the continuing value of the dollar. The hegemonic power of the United States came under challenge, first militarily from the Soviet Union, and, when that collapsed, economically from Germany and Japan. It became clear that the United States deficit had grown too big. It could no longer be allowed to expand; it had indeed to be cut back. Where then would the stimulus for expansion come from? This became an extremely serious question as the world reached a very low level in the economic cycle, when millions are unemployed throughout the industrialized world, and the burden of debt is lowering living standards and holding back development in the Third World.

We are back to the position which Keynes faced 50 years ago. Fortunately, we are not in the middle of a savage war, with dissidents and racial minorities being sent to death camps in the Soviet Union and Germany. But the economic collapse is causing

whole federations of nations to disintegrate, and internecine war
to spread. Keynes's message was clear: no single nation can take
the necessary expansionist steps out of recession on its own. Left
to their own defensive actions nation states are powerless. Even the
largest of them, the United States, in the 1930s, suffered the deepest
slump and the heaviest unemployment. Joint action for economic
expansion is the only way out. The Japanese can spend very large
sums on reflating their economy, because world-wide they have
massive economic surpluses from the exports of their most
competitive industries. The United States can continue for a time
to borrow to cover its deficit, because others, and particularly her
main economic rivals, Germany and Japan, believe that a collapse
there would bring the whole system down. In Europe there is the
mechanism for economic expansion in an Economic and Monetary
Union, but there is a fear of the restrictive policies of the German
bankers as there was before of the United States Treasury. Keynes
believed that the fear was misplaced, if only institutions could be
developed to act internationally in pursuit of expansionist policies
on behalf of all those who decided to act together. Is that once again
a real possibility?

An international money

The balance of power of nation states in the world today is once
more similar to that which Keynes had envisaged in drawing up his
plans for international monetary agreement. It was disturbed by the
devastation and bankruptcy of the war years, which left the United
States in a position of world hegemony, and the Soviet Union in
isolation. Both those disturbances are now ended. The United States
is now the major debtor, along with the UK and many others. Japan
and Germany are now the new creditors along with the oil states,
Switzerland, and the new dragons of East Asia. The need and the
opportunity for a new international monetary agreement is evident.
There is no accepted world money. Gold was abandoned by the
United States as the basis for the dollar way back in 1971. Since
then dollars — called Euro-dollars outside the United States — have
provided a substitute; but the United States foreign account has for
some years been in deep deficit, and the value of the dollar has
declined in relation to other key currencies. Inflation has eroded the
sums available from the IMF and the World Bank, even below what
emerged from Bretton Woods. Small additions have been made in
these funds to take account of rising levels of world trade, but all
countries' total reserves today equal no more than one-fifth of the
value of trade in any year. In 1945, they amounted to nearly 80 per

cent, and in the 1960s to some 50 per cent. The additions have included a minuscule sum added to international credit in line with Keynes's ideas of a world money, through the IMF's creation of SDRs (Special Deposit Reserves). These SDRs have come to be used as a standard against which to measure all other currencies, but they amount to no more than 2 per cent of the world's non-gold reserves.

If the world is crying out for a money that every country can trust in trade outside their frontiers, what is the chance of creating one? Leaders of the G7, the seven strongest economies in the world, meet regularly to co-ordinate policies, but this amounts to nothing more than agreement to reduce inflation and the high level of interest rates. The methods adopted in each of these nation states to achieve these ends are, however, totally counter productive. The governments in each seek, by cutting back on their public expenditure, to reduce purchasing power, and thus the demand both for goods and for borrowing. Having forsworn competitive devaluation of their currencies, they have replaced this with competitive deflation of their economies. The country that reduces its economy to rubble first wins because there will be no demand for goods and nobody wanting to borrow, and the prized goal of nil inflation will have been gained. Of course, all the other countries' economies will have suffered almost as badly, if they have played the same game, partly from their own government's efforts, partly from the intended reduction of imports which are of course some other country's exports. Keynesian policies of expansion are currently out of fashion, because during the boom years of the 1960s and 70s the strength of labour and small scale producers began to threaten the power of capital. The value of money was endangered.

Keynesians, for whom expansion of output was thought to be worth a certain amount of inflation, were replaced as advisers to governments by monetarists, who value money above real output. Inflation has taken the place of unemployment as the enemy to be defeated by economic policy; and the policy has involved weakening the power of workers and small producers to reduce their demands, combined with privatization of public assets and cutting back on public expenditure. Inequality has grown both inside nations and between nations, especially between the more economically advanced and the less. Such a reverse in policy prescription was encouraged by fear of the effect of the increasing scale of United States deficits, both on the national budget and the foreign balance of payments. It was equally encouraged by the fear in Germany, the second most economically powerful state in the world, of any return to the traumatic experience of inflation after two world wars and, as with the USA in the 1940s, by distrust of the spendthrift ways of others who might be encouraged by any sign of expansionist policies in Germany. This fear has been greatly exacerbated by Western Germany's absorbtion of a weak and distorted East German economy on the most generous terms that involve inevitable temporary reduction in West German living standards, and a generally restrictive monetary policy including high interest rates. Only Japan with her huge surplus on overseas account, has been prepared and in a position to take its own measures of domestic economic expansion. Japan, however, shows little sign of being prepared to follow this up with an international initiative, or even to reduce her own protectionist walls against foreign suppliers, except in the case of the basic raw materials that she lacks.

In Europe, the result of this conjuncture of economic and political developments is that the only hope of agreement on international monetary co-operation lies in negotiation with the Germans to achieve a programme of modest expansion under German leadership. This is the kind of bargain Keynes was forced to arrive at in negotiation with the Americans in 1943. It is the kind of bargain that those who favour European monetary co-operation have favoured. The strength of the German economy dominates Europe, and has immense influence throughout the world. It is impossible for countries with economies that are even as large as the UK to put their currencies against the mark. UK interest rates have to follow in line with rates in Germany, and somewhat above the German level, if those who have considerable funds, mainly the large transnational companies, are to keep banking them in pounds sterling. It is better to join a monetary union, and to have some joint influence on German policy through the union, than to try to go back to unilateral management of the currency.

Those who argue most strongly against Britain entering the European Monetary Union say that we don't want to have our economic policy determined by German bankers, and by the movements of the German mark. But that is just what we have now. A European Monetary Union (EMU) would be managed by a European Central Bank operating in ecus. It would be of great importance not to give to the German government the sort of power to influence the Bank that was given to the USA in the case of the IMF and the World Bank. But no one has proposed that, not even the Germans. The proposal is that the Bank should enjoy a large degree of independence of the separate nation states, such as Keynes once hoped to give to the IMF and World Bank. Such is the reputation of those who have managed the affairs of the IMF and the World Bank that such independence is regarded as positively disastrous. But we have made it clear that the IMF and World Bank were in the event never given that independence, and the currency they were operating in was the dollar and not some international bancor or SDR or ecu. It would, of course, be necessary for the European Community through the Parliament and the Commission to set guidelines for the Bank's operations, and to require the Bank to account annually for its activities. Any serious divergence from what should be moderately expansionist goals would necessarily involve the the threat of disciplinary action for the governor, but there would be no question of day to day interference with the Bank's decisions.

A larger budget

It has always been fully understood that a European Monetary Union would need also to be a European Economic Union. The Union would need to have fiscal as well as monetary powers. This would imply a much larger Community budget than exists today, when this is not much more than 2 per cent of the combined national state government budgets of the 12. Without a much larger budget for the Community, there would be no automatic compensation for poorer regions, so that when their income fell their taxes would fall, but Community wide expenditures would continue. There would also need to be much larger funds in the hands of the European Development Bank to meet the needs of the poorer regions. But the key to recovery and expansion would be, as Keynes so well understood, a major pooling of nation state reserves to support what he called a stabilization fund, which could be called upon by states and regions with high levels of unemployment, and deficits in their payment balances. The reserves of states today are only the national computer balances of trade exchanges at any moment; but international agreement to use a proportion of these as collateral for drawing rights would provide the finances of such a fund.

The years of expansionist world policies following on the Bretton Woods agreement were years of maximum growth in the strength of working pople not only in Europe, but throughout the world. If working people benefit most from years of economic expansion, and from what some have called the Age of Equality, then it is time to re-establish the conditions for that happy state.

III
Debt and the Third World

A major element in the expansion of the world economy for three decades following the Bretton Woods agreement was the recovery and continuing rise of world prices for primary commodities — tropical foods and beverages, agricultural materials and minerals. These are the products mainly of the non-industrialized countries, many of which had been colonies of the industrialized countries prior to the Second World War. This had been the artificial division of labour in the world economy that colonial rule had established — primary production in the "South", processing and manufacture in the "North". The recovery of commodity prices in the world's agricultural and mineral markets after the deep slump of the 1930s gave to the primary producing countries immediate access to purchasing power or reserves for future purchases of manufactured goods from the industrialized lands. It was the United States' increasing dependence on outside supplies for the raw materials and fuel of her industries that resulted in the steady outflow of gold from Fort Knox and, then, of Euro-dollars, which kept the post-war boom going. The boom peaked in the early 1970s, with the massive hike not only in the price of oil but also of other minerals.

Since the peaks of the 1970s the prices of primary products have, on average, been halved, while at the same time prices of manufactured goods have doubled. Primary producing countries have been caught in a price scissors. The reason is in part the world-wide recession in industrial activity, in part also the falling proportion of raw materials in the consumption patterns of the industrialized countries. As people's incomes rise they spend more on services and less on goods; and modern industry uses less material per unit of output. All these changes have been reinforced by the development of artificial substitutes to replace natural materials, and by subsidized food production in the industrialized lands — sugar beet and corn syrup, rape and sunflower seed, for example, which have replaced imports from the South of sugar cane and palm oil.

Developing countries that borrowed money in the developed countries during the good years to finance their industrialization programmes and, after the oil price hike, to pay for oil imports if they had no oil reserves themselves, found that they were caught in a debt trap. With their commodity prices falling, they had to export greater volumes to service their debts and, with rising rates of interest, this became more and more difficult. When they borrowed money from the IMF and the World Bank to meet the gap, they were required to step up their exports still further to pay off the debt. They had to run faster and faster just to stay in the same place. As all primary producers were being required to do the same, stocks piled up and prices fell still further. The debt has steadily accumulated and, instead of buying manufactured goods from the industrialized lands, they have to spend up to a third of their export earnings on servicing the debt. Funds on balance have been flowing out of many of the poorest regions rather than the reverse. In many cases the governments of Developing Countries, and especially the Least Developed (LDCs), do not have the funds to invest in new plant and equipment even for their primary production. A few favoured countries in South East Asia are receiving foreign investment in large scale primary production using new cost-saving technologies. In Africa, which has always had the strongest trading links with Europe, foreign investment is being withdrawn. Whole regions are being marginalized (see Table 1). But, for Europe, this can only mean a narrowing of the world market and further unemployment as purchasing power in the Third World declines. Even in 1990 UNCTAD officials were calculating that a cut of just a quarter in debt repayments would restore 70 per cent of the lost capital goods orders from debtor countries, and reduce European unemployment by several percentage points. European governments are rescuing their banks from their Third World debts, but the provisions are not being passed on to the debtor countries.

The ACP countries

Europe has a historic responsibility for the developing countries in the southern hemisphere, which we call the Third World. This is recognised in the Lomé Convention for those countries in Africa, the Caribbean and Pacific (ACP) which were once European colonies. Apart from the Chinese mainland and the Philippines, all the developing countries were once under European colonial rule, continuing outside Latin America right down to the 1940s. With the arguable exceptions of Afghanistan and Haiti, moreover, every one of the 42 countries designated by the United Nations as those 'Least Developed' was once a European colony. These LDCs have populations totalling nearly 400 million. One hundred million are in Bangladesh and 39 million in Burma (Myanmar); the rest mainly in Africa. They comprise 8 per cent of the world's population, but enjoy only 0.7 per cent of total world national income.

Most of these colonies were established to grow one or two particular crops, or to produce one or two minerals for European

Table 1:
Changing Patterns of World Trade, 1980-1989/90

Exports	US$ billions 1980	US$ billions 1990	Percentages 1980	Percentages 1990
A. TRADE BY REGIONS				
World total	2,001	3,387	100	100
Developed total	1,259	2,447	63	72
to Developed	891	1,893	45	56
to Developing	316	472	16	14
Of which OPEC	100	80	5	2
to USSR/E. Europe	42	51	2	1
EEC total	690	1,352	35	40
of which Intra*	387	834	19	25
Extra	303	518	16	15
USA total	217	374	11	11
Canada total	65	127	3	4
EFTA total	112	225	5	7
Japan total	130	287	6	8
Developing total	587	767	29	23
of which OPEC	307	153	15	5
non-OPEC	287	614	14	18
Intra	155	249	8	7
Intra non-OPEC	128	217	6	6
Africa total	95	62	5	2
America total	108	132	5	6
Asia total	162	450	8	13
of which China**	18	61	1	2
USSR/E. Europe total	155	172	8	5
of which Intra	79	66	4	2
B. TRADE BY COMMODITIES				
Manufactures total	1,135	2,181	58	72
of which Chemicals	141	264	7	9
Machinery & Transport	513	1,060	26	36
Other mfg.	481	857	24	26
Fuels	481	292	24	10
Primary Products total	349	501	18	17
of which Food	200	296	10	10
Crude Mats.	149	205	8	7

*Includes FRG-GDR, 1980 — $3b., 1990 — $13b.
**Excludes China trade with Vietnam, Mongolia, N. Korea.

Note: Total Export Values in 1990 = 170% of 1980. Unit Values, for all commodities = 108%, for manufactures = 130% (machinery 148%), for oil = 66%, for food 88%, for agricultural non-food = 100%, for minerals = 71%. Quantum for all = 160%, for manufactures only = 180%.

Source: United Nations Monthly Bulletin of Statistics, June 1991.

consumption. Much of the concentration on a small number of export crops remains characteristic of the least developed countries. But the relative value of their primary products — tropical foods, agricultural raw materials and minerals (apart from fuel oil) — has declined. They take up a smaller proportion now of Europe's final consumption patterns. So the share of the developing countries as suppliers and markets for Western Europe has been reduced. This has amounted, since the Second World War, to a change from around 20 per cent to 15 per cent of Europe's exports and imports (from 13 per cent to 9 per cent for the European Community alone). Africa, which once accounted for about 10 per cent in both cases, is now down to 5 per cent (little more than 3 per cent for the EC). With substitutes for their products increasingly available, and bio-technology likely to increase the range of substitutes, the prospects for the exports of the non-oil producers among the developing countries must seem bleak indeed. Only in the case of certain rare minerals — cobalt, vanadium, tin and diamonds — do some of these countries have a product which the industrialized countries would be hard put to replace.

The increasing concentration of the world's trade in exchanges between the already industrialized countries, as a result of reduced demand and falling prices for the fuel and raw materials of industry previously obtained from the developing countries, is only half the story of trade development in the 1980s. The other half has even greater long-term significance for the developing countries. It is this; that foreign investment by transnational companies from the industrialized countries in plants overseas has been growing much faster than direct exports — at 29 per cent a year in the second half of the 1980s compared with a 9 per cent a year rise in exports in the same period. It is widely supposed that this investment has gone to developing countries, especially in Asia and Latin America, and accounts for the rising scale of imports of manufactured goods that have begun to replace imports of raw materials from these regions. Nothing could be further from the truth. The share of developing countries in the foreign investment flows from the main investing regions — the USA, the EC and Japan — was reduced during the 1980s from 25 per cent of the total to 18 per cent. The proportion of developing countries exports for which the foreign affiliates of US and Japanese firms are responsible is relatively small and has not been growing. Thus both trade and investment is being concentrated in the already developed lands. The increasingly unequal distribution of the world's wealth as a result of these developments must cause any economist of a Keynesian or Marxian persuasion to view the future marketing of the products of this investment with some anxiety — the more so because inequalities of income are also growing rapidly inside the most developed countries.

The world's trade more and more consists of exchanges of industrial goods between industrial countries. There has been some increase in the imports into the most industrialized countries of manufactured goods from developing countries. This has done something to offset the declining share of these countries in the trade of the developed countries; and there has been some increase in the trade between the developing countries themselves. But this intra-trade does not earn them the hard currency which they need to buy the machinery and manufactured goods available only from the industrialized countries. Moreover, while imports of manufactured goods into the industrialized countries from the Third World have appeared to be growing quite fast, these still account for no more than 14 per cent of the total of manufactures entering world trade — an increase from 12 per cent since the 1970s. The share of developing countries in the manufactured imports of the main industrialized regions, the USA and Canada, the EC and Japan, is higher at around 25 per cent; but, as a proportion of the total home market of these countries, this contribution from the non-industrialized regions amounts to no more than a rise from 3 per cent to 4 per cent.

The 'little dragons'

Only a small number of developing countries have succeeded in establishing themselves securely in the world market for manufactures. The chief of these are the four so-called 'little dragons' of the Far East — Hong Kong, Singapore, South Korea and Taiwan. The first two are chiefly enterprise zones processing materials received from outside as part of the synergy of giant transnational companies, but South Korea and Taiwan have established their own independent large-scale enterprises. They have done this through original equipment manufacturing (OEM) arrangements, that is to say, long-term subcontracting to supply components and sub-assembles for giant manufacturing companies not only in Japan but also in the United States. This has not involved much direct investment from outside, but has permitted them over a period of time to engender their own capital accumulation. The contrast with the policies followed by European companies in Africa and the other ACP countries could hardly be greater. As a result of these policies and the support given to them by the European Community, the developing countries for which Europe has most responsibility have signally failed to get any purchase on the processing of their raw material resources. Apart from the 'little dragons' and some of the larger developing countries, the one-time colonies of Europe remain with very little more industrial employment than they had forty years ago.

Three reasons for the continued lack of development in the so-called 'developing countries' can be said to be the result of European actions. First, money was lent for development, to be repaid with commodities; but interest rates were raised and, as debts grew and more commodities were produced for export, commodity prices fell. Some funds have been made available from European Community budgets to offset the price declines of ACP producers through STABEX, SYMEX and similar schemes, but the sums involved have been relatively small. An actual reverse flow of funds back from the developing countries to the developed took place, and, although this was checked as the result of rescheduling arrangements, the actual size of the debt continues to grow. Second, Europe has maintained protectionist policies against imports from the Third World — not only to support its own agricultural producers of grains and sugar and meat, but also to protect its manufacturers, through escalating tariffs rising according to the degree of processing involved. These apply to imports from ACP countries in the case of coffee, cocoa, sisal, fruit, and oil seed products. They are much more serious for non-ACP countries seeking to export their processed products to Europe.

There are many fears in the developing countries, including those in the ACP group, that from 1992 the Single Market will mean even more protection of the European market, as the discriminating support of individual Community members for the agricultural products of their ex-colonies is phased out. Some ACP producers that have had protected markets in Europe, for example for bananas, will be less able to compete with much larger scale producers. This is only one aspect of the supplanting of small-scale farming by agri-business everywhere. The European Community has taken steps to protect its small farmers as well as the big ones; but similar protection provided by Third World governments to their farmers is regarded by World Bank advisors as perverse and a disqualification for receipt of aid. Yet, in terms of soil conservation and environmental protection, as well as of providing local employment, it is small-scale farming that is the most beneficial. Protection of agriculture in the early stages of industrialization is now accepted as an essential element in economic growth — in South Korea as in Great Britain in its industrial revolution. But this is no argument for continuing protection in industrialized countries.

Complaints from the Third World about the other obstacles that are placed by Europeans in the way of the advance of the developing countries may be regarded as even more controversial. They all refer to the role of the giant transnational companies that control the markets for almost all of the commodities produced for export in developing countries. It is bad enough for these countries that the prices of their primary products have been falling relative to those of manufactured goods; but what is worse is that such a small proportion even of that price actually stays in the producing country. This is partly because the processing takes place outside, as we have seen, but it is also because the ownership of mines and plantations is in European or North American hands. As a result profits are remitted outside the developing countries concerned, and the transfer pricing systems of large companies, combined with their use of tax havens for registering their subsidiary companies, leads to the creaming off of a very large part of the value of the original primary product. What is left for a developing country government to tax is quite a small part, and the taxes on exports and other taxes imposed have led to complaints from World Bank officials of excessive rent seeking.

One of the objectives of international aid for developing countries has been to offset by contributions from the whole industrialized world community some of the loss incurred by developing countries from the actions of individual European and North American interests that have been detailed above. Unfortunately, during the 1980s when developing countries were suffering most from falling prices and rising debt payments, overseas development assistance (ODA) from developed countries failed to rise in real terms, and fell steadily as a proportion of developed countries' national income (GDP). On average, the proportion for all developed countries fell below one half of the 0.7 per cent ODA/GDP ratio set by the UN for aid to the least developed countries. Only Norway, Netherlands, Denmark, Sweden and Finland achieved the target figure. Most worrying for the developing countries, and especially for the least developed ACP countries, is the fear that the direction of measures of financial assistance from Western Europe will shift sharply from the Third World to Eastern Europe. Bold promises that this would not happen have been belied by events. There are evident pressures on the German government, but the opening up of investment opportunities in Eastern Europe for private investment from all parts of the Community is bound to be in competition with the claims of the Third World.

Possibilities

Rather than thinking solely in terms of aid and investment, this chapter is designed to direct attention to the possibilities of increasing trade between Europe and the developing countries, and of increasingly incorporating Eastern Europe and the republics of the former Soviet Union into the trade of Western Europe with the rest of the world. The trade of developing countries (DCs) with what were the centrally planned economies (CPEs) of Eastern Europe, the Soviet Union and China has always been of rather more importance for the CPEs than for the DCs. For the developing countries it has amounted to around 10% of imports and exports. For the CPEs it has amounted to nearly twice this figure, and there has been a particularly marked growth in CPE imports of manufactured goods from newly industrializing countries. This is mainly accounted for by exports from Asian countries to China. There has been some limited growth of such trade with Eastern Europe and the former Soviet Union. This trade is reduced by the fact that both DCs and CPEs suffer equally from the burden of debts and look to earning hard currency from their exports.

In what way, then, could Eastern Europe and the republics of the former Soviet Union be incorporated into the trade of Western Europe and the developing countries? The former Soviet Union has all the minerals required for industrial production with the exception of tin, which is available in China, and she has all the other raw materials for manufacturing such as timber and cotton and other fibres. What she and the Eastern European countries undoubtedly need is machinery and modern technology from the west. But they also need consumer goods to provide the incentive for increased production, especially in agriculture. These comprise not only manufactured goods, which are increasingly entering world trade from the newly industrializing countries, but also tropical and semi-tropical foods and beverages. Tea and tobacco are grown in the former Soviet Union as well as a limited quantity of citrus fruits, soya and sugar (though Eastern Europe has relied mainly on Cuba for its sugar). Coffee and cocoa cannot be grown in the former USSR, nor can palm oil or any of the tropical fruits — bananas, pineapples, peanuts and other tropical nuts — or green vegetables and apples in the northern winter. The opportunities for increased sales of coffee in Eastern Europe and the former Soviet Union, including the robusta coffee from Africa, appear to be very good. In exchange, the republics of the former Soviet Union could offer oil to the non-oil producing developing countries, and Eastern Europe could supply some of the intermediate technology that many of the least developed countries are in need of. It is here that a possible triangle of trade development presents itself: advanced machinery and technical know-how from Western Europe to the East, oil and intermediate technology from the East to the South, and mineral and tropical products from the South to Western Europe as well as the East.

Major steps

Three major steps have to be taken to make a reality of such trade development. The first necessity is some relaxation of the present restrictions on imports into Europe of the more highly processed products of developing countries and an end to food "dumping" under the Common Agricultural Policy. Secondly, it would be necessary to find means of financing increased trade exchanges between the Third World and the countries of Eastern Europe and the Soviet Union, which, as we have seen, all share the same desperate need to direct all their exports to earning hard currency to pay their debts to the industrialized countries. The third requirement would have to be found together with the supply of finance for trade development. This would be the establishment of a trade development organization of the kind that Keynes originally proposed at the Bretton Woods meetings, which was, as we have seen, replaced by the General Agreement on Tariffs and Trade (GATT) in the form of a purely negotiating and monitoring body. It would be concerned to create new networks of trade exchanges and to assist with product development and marketing. It could make use of the East Asian experience of original equipment manufacturing arrangements as well as of the experience of non-governmental organizations in the transfer of intermediate technology. A prototype for such an organization has for long been under discussion between ACP representatives and non-governmental organizations under the terms of the fourth Lomé Convention. If it proves to be successful, it could be generalized to establish trade exchanges that would link the European Community with Eastern Europe and the Third World in a whole new order of fair trade and sustainable development.[1]

If moral and ecological arguments about what is fair and sustainable fail to impress, there is a further argument that has seemed in the past to be a powerful consideration for those who live in relative affluence in the industrialized countries. This argument was deployed to some effect, but evidently not enough, in the Brandt Reports on *North-South*: the *Programme for Survival* and the *Common Crisis*. This was the argument, now starkly relevant, that economic misery generates conflict and disorder and even war, which cannot be limited to internecine struggles in the Third World, but can easily spread.[2] The emergence of dictators and the recourse to military solutions to problems have always been associated with economic recession and with the frustration of rising popular expectations of better times. It must be a paramount lesson that economic adversity through debt and decline in one part of the world cannot be allowed to remain unattended without the resultant common crisis enveloping the whole world.

References to Part II
The main source drawn upon is R.N. Gardner, *Sterling-Dollar Diplomacy*, Oxford, 1956. Other books consulted include: Roy Harrod, *Life of J.M. Keynes*, Macmillan, 1963; Correlli Barnett, *The Audit of War*, Macmillan, 1986; H.W. Arndt, *Economic Lessons of the 1930s*, Oxford, 1944; Michael Barratt Brown, *After Imperialism*, Heinemann, 1963; Stanley W. Black, *A Levite among the Priests: Edward M.Bernstein and the Origins of the Bretton Woods System*, Woodview Press 1991. Statistical material is taken mainly from IMF, *International Financial Statistics, Yearbooks*. Some further proposals on European Monetary Union can be found in: Michael Barratt Brown, *European Union: Fortress or Democracy?*, Spokesman for European Labour Forum, 1991.

References to Part III
1. For a full development of this argument see M. Barratt Brown, *Fair Trade: Reforming the International Trading System*, Zed Books, 1993.
2. It has been rehearsed with much supporting evidence by Susan George *et al* in *The Debt Boomerang: How Third World Debt Harms us All*, Pluto Press and TNI, 1992.

CHAPTER 5

The Scope and Limits of Community Action

Jacques Delors

The President of the European Commission answered questions from the European Parliament's Socialist Group.

The world economy

How do you see the economic situation in the Community in relation to the world economy?

. . . In spite of the progress made, the European Community has not achieved sufficient growth or autonomy. It is amazing to see all our finance ministers looking at the indicators every day in the United States. And that must be a major lesson for us. We are not yet capable of giving impetus to the world economy. When the world economy is strong and growing, we add something. I think we will soon be able to bring you an evaluation of the Cecchini report, and we can see that the 1992 objective has added to the growth. But when there is a slow-down of activity in the USA, plus a purge in Great Britain, and in the Community, while Japan is closed in upon itself; well, we will never get there . . . Clearly, we have not yet got the necessary strength to carry out an economic policy that can also bring relief to others . . .

. . . When the G7 meets again, it will discuss matters which concern 800 million people in the world. But we are really 5.5 billion, world-wide. The other 4.7 billion do not participate in the world economy, but they suffer from it. There is monetary instability and there are high rates of interest. Who pays the bill? We do. But they pay even more than we do. Look at the unsatisfactory allocation of financial resources — in 1990, 50 billion dollars were transferred from debtor to creditor countries. Commercial protectionism — who suffers from it the most? They do! Hence the necessity for a good relationship with GATT . . .

You will recall that in the 19th century, in the early days of industrial society, the bourgeoisie became rich. It was a very creative period. Then, at one point, the bourgeoisie said to itself: "Yes, but production must not grow any more." Why? Because wage-earners, workers, did not have a place, and there was this economic and social revolution, from the creation of trade unions to Keynes, which brought us to understand that if, in a particular community, money is not properly distributed, growth is halted. It is the same problem we face today, at this stage in the world's development, though nobody talks about it.

Budgets

What significance has the common budget of the Community as an instrument of economic policy?

We must bear in mind one figure. In 1997, Community expenditure will represent only 3 per cent of the total public expenditure of the member states. I myself had calculated the necessary amount at 5 per cent in the framework of economic and monetary union, and in the framework of subsidiarity, properly applied . . .

. . . As far as economic and monetary union and public debt are concerned, I will repeat Bernstein's famous formula, which you all know: "the movement is everything, the goal is nothing" . . . If the criteria are applied too rigidly, then in my opinion we will never have economic and monetary union. Mr von der Vring tells me that budgetary discipline is not great enough. That is true, but I am going to tell you a little story that I hope will not shock you. I have proposed that in the Delors 2 package we leave out 300 budgetary lines that are less than 10 million ecus. My colleagues have said this is impossible; 200 of these lines were proposed by Parliament. I leave you to think about this! . . .

. . . The level of investment is one of the greatest difficulties of Delors 2. To get the system going is just as difficult as to try to change the direction of a 50 million tonne petrol tanker, because we have to give regard to what is equitable. The country that was treated least equitably was undoubtedly Spain. In order to treat Spain better, we would have had to start again from a zero budget, taking account of the respective impact of large items of expenditure and also of the system of receipts.

But I would like to draw your attention to the fact that there is not a single federal state in the world where the level of financial transfers made to certain countries is so high. In other words, we were able to attain net transfers for two countries in 1987 of the order of 8 per cent of their gross national product. You don't find that anywhere. To be sure, Federal Germany intends to review its base system after four or five years' effort towards unification, to try to find a method of gradual progress. This is particularly for the new East German Länder, which I would point out we have put in Objective 1 (for Structural Fund assistance). That is a very important political decision . . .

How do we know what the supplementary cost is, and what represents a transfer from national budgets to the Community budget?

We can consider that of the 22 billion ecus extra expenditure, (even if this is only 21 billion net), 11 billion cover cohesion and are extra expenditure, and 11 billion ecus cover transfers from the national budget to the Community budget, including those for the CAP, for competitiveness, and for external relations. When a finance minister tells me "you are proposing 30 per cent extra," I say "no". We are proposing 15 per cent more in respect of our obligations for economic and social cohesion, and this is extra money we are asking from our citizens. And we propose 15 per cent more for expenditure which you will do at the national level. So it is not 30 per cent extra, as some countries are saying . . .

. . . A year ago, taking account of the situation of the building trade and public works in our countries, if the finance ministers had been willing, but they were not, it was possible to borrow 2 billion ecus within the Community in order to stimulate the programmes in the building industry and public works. In no way would that have been inflationary. It would not have increased the countries' debts, since it would have been the Community that was borrowing. But such things are not in fashion . . .

Social and cohesion funds

What are the respective roles of the social fund and the cohesion fund?

The structural policies are concerned with relations between the regions, and the criteria are the development of each region. The cohesion funds are concerned with relations between nations. They are added to the relations between the regions.

The four countries whose national wealth is lower than 90 per cent of the Community average can lay claim to the cohesion funds. There are two conditions for this, and only two. It is simple, and I hope my colleagues will not complicate it. Firstly, the country must have put forward a programme of convergence, within the framework of Economic and Monetary Union accepted by the Council of Ministers. Secondly, there must be community-based programmes on the environment or on the infrastructure that involve excessive costs for these countries.

If these two conditions are met, the cohesion funds will come into play and must operate in a sensitive way from 1993, when

Package 2 is adopted. But to give you an idea of the scale, the increase in expenditure of structural funds over that period is of the order of 100 to 110 billion ecus. The cohesion funds will come to 10 billion ecus, and will mean that we start to treat some countries, notably Spain, more equitably, and help to make the networks of infrastructure a reality . . .

Industry and research

What is your opinion of the Community's research programme?

. . . We must be aware of the power relationships within the European Council and within the Commission. It was very difficult to get the proposal on competition passed, since there are some people who fear industrial policy in the pejorative sense of state subsidies for business. There are the English who think there is no need to have European champions. That is one of Jacques Delors' absurd ideas. And then there are even socialists who think we must help both small and large businesses. If we develop a common European foreign policy and lack control of electronics, information technology, nuclear fusion and other things, I do not see what we will be able to say in the world. But the power relationships are not simple. For example, it was a terrible battle to get agreement on the text for industrial policy. There was one head of government who banged the table, saying it was unacceptable, absurd . . .

. . . Regarding research, at the time the ESPRIT programme was launched, it was a great success. It created an arena in Brussels to which all the researchers came, whether from business or the universities. But, today, the ESPRIT programme is threatened, in the same way that regional funds were prior to the first budget package. That is to say, there are too many projects. And, it must be said, too many civil servants feeling they have the power because they have money to distribute.

So we need to change the system by means of two forms of action. One form is 'top down' actions, corresponding to large projects such as nuclear fusion, which must continue. The other is 'bottom up' projects coming from businesses, which must not simply be confined to the pre-competitive domain. And there the question is to know whether governments, the commissioners in charge, and the civil servants will accept this change in attitude. If they do not, I predict a decline in the level of funds for research.

I am sure the policy on research has been successful. But it must be fundamentally adapted. Let me give an example. The five Japanese car businesses, at the instigation of MITI, are working together to try to find a car which is completely suitable, to try to increase driving safety and to focus on new materials. The rules of the game are simple: the day they are successful, each one will take the new invention, and may the best man win. I called together the four leading car firms in France and asked them "what are you collaborating on?" "Nothing, almost nothing," was the reply. So, consequently, if they get together and come and tell us: "Here you are. We are researching a suitable car. It will cost 10 billion ecus over 5 years. We will put in 5 billion ecus. National programmes will put in 3 billion ecus. That leaves a gap of 2 billion." The figures are too high, but it is an example. "Will you put this in?" "Oh yes." But the English will say: "There is no English car business. You must give it to Toyota in Great Britain as well." We will refuse, because that is bad industrial policy. If we lose that battle, we have decided to go along with the decline of the Community.

But there is widespread resistance. First of all, there is an incorrect interpretation of what I say. If, in the midst of all my activities, I take time to see all the big industrialists, it is to try to understand their needs. It is the same as with the car manufacturers. The average age of the workers in the four businesses is 47. There are no replacements coming up. One-third of them only know how to read and write, and are thus incapable of adapting themselves to the new way of working "just in time". They are capable of making something, because they are all good mechanics. It is a training effort that represents, in these four businesses, 2 billion ecus over 5 years. This will not happen unless the Community takes the initiative. So a time will come when the Community, by meeting 10 or 20 per cent of the cost, can allow an operation to take place. Will they do it? Or will Great Britain once again come and say: "Oh no, that's a socialist type of industrial policy and, what's more, a French socialist one, and we cannot accept that. There is no reason why Toyota should not have the money as well." It is the same for training.

So the question is to know whether the Commission can have more room to manoeuvre, once the principle is accepted, and the Commission has more responsibility in relation to the European Council and the European Parliament. But, in the present state of affairs, we can do nothing. It's the same for the regulations concerning structural funds for regional policy. Our hands are tied in every sphere. If I go to Italy, I am asked why hard wheat there is subsidized, while 15 kilometres away it is not. I reply that it is all to do with statistics. At present, statistics are the greatest political idiocy. We need to change this. If we don't, the system will not function and, gradually, we will come to a system of pure financial transfer, which will be calculated in a miserly way. But we will not have any coherent economic sphere. . .

What about the social dimension?

. . . I think we have the means to create in the Community a legal safety net for all workers so as to avoid social dumping, without overburdening the business enterprises of the less developed member states. But I think, if you were in agreement, we could go into the subject in more depth so as to create a social dynamic at European level. If it is the Parliament and the Directive that try to do it all, we do not create this social dynamic, and we do not help the European trade union movement to find its role and presence in the Community. On the other hand, the Economic and Social Committee can equally be very useful . . .

What can be done for training?

. . . We would obviously like to do more. But the credits we have for employment and training policy represent 3 per cent of total expenditure from the member states. With this amount, we cannot do more than help the underdeveloped regions. That is, help structural policies and also come to the aid of business competitiveness. This is, in any case, among objectives one and five of the structural funds for regional aid. Objectives three and four are those that have been least successful as they have been targeted. Why? Because programmes for young people's access to the labour market and the struggle against long-term unemployment have been, in general, diverted by national treasuries to obtain a share of the money. And in these cases we have not had satisfactory programmes. But if we want to do more, then we must increase these credits . . .

Poverty

What can done about poverty and inequality?

. . . I do not believe that financial stability is an obstacle to social progress. The example of Germany shows the contrary. But as far as poverty is concerned, it is at the moment a problem of national character. We have a pilot programme to make people think, to make them aware of the sequence of events; impossibility of getting into the job market or of getting out of it, marginalization, poverty, or, indeed, awareness of the pattern of excessive urban development, banishment of the less wealthy to the periphery, social problems, and violence. The Community has to make the nations aware of these two questions. But it does not have the political or financial means to resolve them. It is a huge problem, and the Community can, from time to time, come up with new ideas to make the member states more aware. But I repeat that, in the end, the Community is doing too many things and so it will end up doing them badly. I am sure of that.

At the moment, we have eleven priorities and we are doing badly in some of these areas. It cannot be otherwise. And we need to distinguish more clearly what is essential for the Community in its role of creating an organized economic sphere, working towards economic and monetary union, having a common foreign policy on subjects of vital interest, having good coherence between foreign policy and foreign economic relations, which is far from being established. That is the role of the Community. The rest is for the nation states or the regions and Länder.

For 20 per cent of its time, the Community can retain the capability for raising awareness and innovation. It is in this perspective that there could be action by the Community to draw attention to the serious problems of poverty existing within the Community, which will not be resolved by the present structural policies. But the question of inequalities of poverty is so deeply ingrained in our society that it implies a task of intellectual thought and, perhaps, a political initiative by the Community to make the member countries face their responsibilities . . .

Enlargement

How do you view expansion of the Community?

. . . It seems to me that the requirements of the Community, or the requirements of Europe, are much greater than one might think. In addition to the European agreements we are at present drawing up, thought must be given to the architecture of Europe as a whole. This includes the political response the people expect, particularly the Eastern and Central European countries, and also the Mediterranean ones. We need to think about all that. We have intervened to a large extent. We are the ones who are paying the most. But we are not thinking globally. It is very interesting to see that intellectuals from all the European countries were not interested in building Europe until the fall of the Berlin Wall. They are interested now. And they are urging us to tell them if we have any ideas about how to reconstruct this Europe, taking account of peace, freedom, and justice. Well, we don't have this major idea yet . . .

. . . At the moment, if we take Europe without the former Soviet Union republics, but include the Baltic countries, there could be 35 countries in the Community. If that were the case, everything we have been talking about would have to be drastically reviewed.

That is where thinking about the architecture is useful. For example, Poland, Czechoslovakia, and Hungary, in spite of my advice, look upon Europe solely in terms of their bilateral relations with the Community. They do not co-operate with each other. As a result, they are asking the Community to welcome their entire production, and, as COMECON has broken up, 60 per cent of their trade has collapsed. We have been telling them to work together, and that is why my suggestion is — I don't know if it will work — to propose to the six East European countries, including Bulgaria, Romania, and Albania, that they form a European monetary union in order to stimulate their trade . . .

What help is available for Eastern Europe and the Mediterranean?

. . . In Package 2 we made an arbitrary calculation of the necessary resources. Why arbitrary? Because we don't know. We put the figure high enough not to disappoint the Eastern and Southern countries, but not so high as to attract the whole world's envy. But, in my opinion, consideration of the Mediterranean and the East has only just begun. In the present state of affairs, we do not yet have the corpus of thought which would allow me to tell you today that the Community is in a position to play a part in the matter of peace and development in these countries.

Despite the disadvantages, it is we who make 80 per cent of the efforts to give aid to Eastern and Central European countries, and 80 per cent of the technical assistance to Russia. But, in spite of that, I am not satisfied, and that calls for fundamental consideration. This can only exist if the common foreign policy takes shape. That is, there are no improvisations. A Minister for Foreign Affairs arrives at a meeting and says: '. . . and if we made a conversion centre for atomic scientists . . .', or another says, '. . . if we made a free exchange zone with Morocco . . .' This is complete improvisation. There is no comprehensive consideration, because they are not yet accustomed to working as they do in their own chancellery, that is, having the culture, the historical knowledge, the geographical knowledge . . .

CHAPTER 6

Economic and Monetary Union and the European Community Budget

Sir Donald MacDougall

In 1977 the European Commission published the report of a Study Group that it had set up, under my Chairmanship, on "The Role of Public Finance in European Integration". This is sometimes called the "MacDougall Report", which does scant justice to my six European colleagues, our two consultants from the United States and Australia, and our excellent Secretariat.

It was based to a considerable extent on a study of eight existing economic and monetary unions — five federations (the United States, Canada, West Germany, Switzerland, Australia) and three unitary states (France, Italy, and the United Kingdom). Although it was most unlikely that the European Community would be anything like so fully integrated for many years to come, we believed that our analysis would help to throw light on how its public finance activities might be expanded and improved over a shorter period of time.

The Report is still quite frequently referred to, but there is sometimes a little confusion about what it actually said. It may therefore be useful, before going on to discuss its implications for the future of European integration, to summarize some of our relevant findings and conclusions (to which I shall add, in parentheses, a few comments by way of amplification or justification).

1. Public expenditure by the members of the Community (then nine in number) was about 45 per cent of the GDP of the area as a whole. Expenditure by the Community was 0.7 per cent. In the federal countries we studied, public expenditure by the Federal Government, as distinct from that at lower levels, was around 20-25 per cent of GDP.

2. *Per capita* incomes were at least as unequal[1] between the nine member states of the Community, and between the 72 regions we distinguished in the Community, as they were on average between the various regions of the countries we studied, even *before*

allowing for the equalizing effects of public expenditure and taxation. (The subsequent admission of Spain, Greece and Portugal will have tended to reinforce this conclusion.)

3. In the countries studied, public expenditure and taxation *reduced* regional inequalities in *per capita* incomes by, on average, about 40 per cent so that, after allowing for the effects of public finance — which helped poorer regions at the expense of richer ones — there was much *less* geographical inequality within the existing economic unions than there was within the Community, whose budget, besides being very small, had a weak redistributive effect per ECU spent and received.

4. In unitary states a large part of the total redistribution between regions arose automatically and was in a sense "invisible"; high incomes went with high tax payments and low incomes with relatively high receipts of centrally provided services and transfer payments. In federal countries, inter-governmental grants and tax-sharing played a much more important part. These achieved relatively large redistributive results with relatively small amounts of federal expenditure, because the net inter-regional transfers were to a smaller extent than in the unitary countries the result of differences between large gross payments in opposite directions.

5. As well as redistributing income regionally on a continuing basis, public finance in existing EMUs played a major role in cushioning short-term fluctuations. For example, we reckoned that one-half to two-thirds of a loss of income in a region due to a fall in its external sales was automatically offset through lower payments of taxes and insurance contributions to the centre and higher receipts of unemployment and other benefits. There was no such mechanism in operation on any significant scale between member countries of the Community.

6. Even with the powerful regional effects of public finance just described, several countries had only with difficulty been able to avoid intolerable tensions arising from regional disparities in levels of employment, living standards and rates of growth. (Such disparities can arise despite migration from the depressed to the more prosperous regions, which can itself cause further problems: congestion, and possibly resentment, in the latter regions; and, in the former, waste or under-utilization of the capital stock, both public and private, including housing. A vicious downward spiral may also develop if the younger, more enterprising and more skilful people leave; and if this, coupled with lower demand in the areas, discourages private investment, while local public investment is reduced through loss of local revenue.)

Increasing the Community Budget

On the basis of the above, and other much more detailed information, and taking account of what we assumed to be political realities, we suggested, as a first step, an increase in the Community Budget over, say, the following decade or so, from 0.7 per cent to around 2-2½ per cent of GDP. This would begin to exploit the case for Community involvement where there were economies of scale, or "spill-over" from one part of the Community to others, or indeed to all of it. An important example of the latter would be Community action, particularly in the areas of regional, unemployment and manpower policies, to ensure so far as possible that the benefits of closer integration were seen to accrue to all, that there was a narrowing — or at least not a widening — of the disparities between the economic performances and fortunes of member states. The aim of these measures would be mainly, but not only, to reduce inter-regional differences in capital endowment and productivity, and so help poorer areas to improve their economic performance, rather than to increase, by mere subsidization, their levels of private and public consumption. We reckoned that our proposals would reduce inequalities in *per capita* incomes between members by about 10 per cent.

We were also aware that most governments were reluctant to see any significant increase in public expenditure at all levels — Community, national, state and local — as a percentage of GDP. We therefore looked for desirable transfers of expenditure from national to Community level, for example, external aid programmes, high technology research, and a suggested Community Unemployment Fund;[2] for savings in existing expenditure, notably agriculture; for the most cost-effective methods of achieving the objectives — there was much to be learned from the experience of existing federations; and avoidance of regulations, harmonization, and so on, which were not worthwhile in terms of the extra bureaucratic and compliance costs involved (a matter to which I sometimes wonder whether the Community pays sufficient attention). We reckoned that Community expenditure would not be increased by more than 1 per cent of GDP, and hoped that this could be offset by the economies in national expenditures then being sought. We suggested that the additional Community revenue involved might be raised in part by a more progressive system.

We did not, however, believe that the relatively modest Community budget we were proposing would be nearly sufficient to sustain a monetary union. It need not be anything like as high as the average of around 45 per cent of GDP in the EC member states, or even the 20-25 per cent of federal expenditure in the federal states we studied. We judged that a Community budget of the order of 5-7 per cent might just suffice (or 7½-10 per cent if defence were included), *if, but only if,* it concentrated much more than in existing federations on the cushioning of temporary fluctuations and the geographical equalization of productivity and living standards.

The budget we proposed in this context would have reduced geographical inequalities by some 40 per cent, as, on average, in the countries we studied. We reckoned, it is true, in a purely hypothetical simulation, that using entirely a mechanism similar to the German *Länderfinanzausgleich,* which involved direct transfers between the *Länder,* a 40 per cent reduction in inequalities between the nine member states in 1975 could have been achieved by unconditional transfers to the governments of the three poorer countries from those of the six richer ones of amounts equivalent to only 2 per cent of Community GDP. But we regarded a Community budget consisting entirely, or even mainly, of such a scheme as quite unrealistic. There are, quite rightly, bound to be objectives other than geographical equalization, and gross Community revenues and expenditure are almost certain to be much larger than net transfers. (It is interesting that the 1992 Community budget is about five times as large as the total of the transfers from the net contributing countries to the net recipients.)

Since 1977 the budget has increased from 0.7 per cent of GDP in the Community to 1.2 per cent in 1992, and the Commission's proposals following Maastricht would increase it to around 1.35 per cent in 1997. But this would mean an increase of nearly one-third in Community expenditure and is, perhaps not surprisingly, strongly opposed by many member states. It would, however, still fall short of our modest 'interim' proposal of 2-2½ per cent, and is of a different order of magnitude from what our Group felt, and I still feel, would be necessary to sustain monetary union. (I would not go to the stake for our precise figure of 5-7 per cent, but it seems not unreasonable to suggest that, if a budget of 2-2½ per cent is required to reduce geographical inequality by 10 per cent, one of at least twice that size would be needed to achieve a 40 per cent reduction. Our suggested Community Budget would, moreover, be only about one-quarter of the federal budgets in existing federations, as a proportion of GDP.)

Cushioning fluctuations

I also think that, in the context of a monetary union, a much larger

Community Budget than is at present contemplated would be necessary to cushion the effects of short-term (and medium-term) fluctuations, as was done in existing EMUs. Even if the rate of inflation in a country was among the lowest in the Community, and even if its *per capita* income was similar to that in the Community as a whole, it might run into difficulties because, for example, its products lost out to substitutes, or it became over-dependent on declining industries. Without help from the Community, whether automatic or deliberate, it might then, having lost the power to vary its exchange rate, have to suffer a prolonged period of painful adjustment, with sluggish, or even negative, economic growth, high unemployment, and possibly outward migration with the associated problems described earlier.[3] With a single currency, while national balance of payments problems as we have known them would no longer exist, they would be replaced by this kind of suffering. It could, and should, be mitigated by temporary Community assistance, including help with the structural changes that are required. These take time to be effective, and one cannot rely on rapid changes in relative costs and prices, which tend to be notoriously sticky in industrial countries.

Many, however, would challenge this argument on the ground that exchange-rate changes are of little value, so that the loss of the power to use them is no great sacrifice. I would dispute this, first of all by quoting from the Report of the Delors Committee on economic and monetary union[4] (whose members included, in addition to the President of the European Commission, twelve Presidents or Governors of central banks and the Managing Director of the Bank for International Settlements). They said: 'The permanent fixing of exchange rates would deprive individual countries of an important instrument for the correction of economic imbalances'.[5]

I too believe that, in the medium term at least, exchange-rate changes can be a valuable weapon, when used in conjunction with appropriate fiscal and monetary policies. Whatever some economic models may now suggest, there are numerous historical experiences to support this view. One is what happened after the devaluation of sterling in November 1967, and the complementary measures taken during the following few months to restrain domestic demand. 1968 was a difficult year, partly because of the so-called 'J-curve', which means that devaluation tends to worsen the balance of payments before improving it. But by the summer of 1969 it was clear that there had been a sharp turnround in the balance of payments, and a classic shift of resources: a very large increase in exports coupled with a much smaller rise in imports, a large increase in manufacturing investment, hardly any rise in consumers' expenditure and a fall in public consumption. More recently, there was a close correlation in the 1980s, in the United States and Japan, between changes in their real effective exchange rates (measured by relative unit labour costs) and their current accounts; and between their nominal and real effective exchange rates.[6]

As the latter correlation suggests, it is wrong to think that the beneficial effects of devaluation will always be wiped out quite quickly by faster inflation. For example, after the devaluation of sterling against the dollar by about 30 per cent in 1949, the United Kingdom retained virtually all the competitive advantage gained *vis-à-vis* the United States for four to five years, and the bulk of it for considerably longer.[7]

It will also be argued that a much larger Community budget is not required to support monetary union since what really matters is 'convergence' in terms of rates of inflation, interest rates, exchange-rate stability, government borrowing and debt. The degrees of convergence required in these fields to qualify for membership of the monetary union are defined precisely in the Maastricht Treaty. Most may well be necessary conditions but they are not, in my view, sufficient. I would regard as equally important the achievement of economic and social 'cohesion', an objective referred to only in rather general terms in the Treaty.

Here again I would quote from the Delors Report[8] (italics mine):

'If sufficient consideration were not given to *regional imbalances*, the economic union would be faced with *grave economic and political risks*'. 'The economic and monetary union would have to encourage and guide *structural adjustment which would help poorer regions to catch up with the wealthier ones*'. 'Policies should be geared to price stability, *balanced growth, converging standards of living, high employment*'. The Committee evidently recognized the danger of the Community becoming what I have heard described as a 'low growth, high unemployment club'.

The Delors Report, in my view, thus gave most of the arguments for a much larger Community budget to sustain monetary union. It implies clearly that the necessary cohesion will not occur of its own accord. The excellent report by the National Institute for Economic and Social Research to the European Parliament on 'A new strategy for social and economic cohesion after 1992' makes a powerful case for stronger policies to this end by the Community. It paints a worrying picture of the outlook for many of the less prosperous regions (and of areas, hitherto relatively prosperous, but likely to lose ground — and these could well include substantial parts of the United Kingdom); and of the possible adverse effects on them, relative to the rest of the Community, not only of the Single Internal Market and the transition to Economic and Monetary Union, but of a number of other unrelated developments likely to occur in the 1990s.

The Report, no doubt realistically, assumes that only a small increase in the Community budget, as a percentage of GDP, is likely to be politically acceptable over the next five years or so. But it also considers the possibility of more ambitious programmes, and discusses a number of possible measures that seem to the authors unlikely to be acceptable in the foreseeable future, either for political reasons or because they would involve excessive demands on Community funds. Some of these might become feasible at a later date, for political attitudes change — and may indeed need to change if the degree of integration hoped for by many, including a single currency, is to be achieved. The Report recognises too that its recommendations go only part of the way to achieving the necessary degree of cohesion, and proposes that later in the decade there should be a thorough examination of possible mechanisms for more substantial inter-regional redistribution, as explored in the 'MacDougall Report'. I sincerely hope that this will be done, because I fear that an attempt to introduce monetary union without a much larger Community budget than at present would run the risk of setting back, rather than promoting, progress towards closer integration in Europe.

Our Study Group considered that the experience of existing monetary unions provided a reasonably objective yardstick for the degree of regional equality required to support such a union — in modern jargon, for what 'cohesion' would involve in quantitative terms. If it is argued that greater regional inequality, whether temporary or permanent, could be tolerated in a European monetary union, and that a much smaller Community budget would be required than the one we suggested, I would once again point out that it was only about one-quarter the size of that in existing federations, as a percentage of GDP.

I am attracted by the possibility, discussed in the National Institute Report, that the European Investment Bank (EIB) might make a much greater contribution to the achievement of cohesion. EIB loans for regional development are already of the same order as grants from the structural funds for this purpose. The provision of 'soft' loans (subsidized by the Community), and possibly of venture capital, might make a substantial additional contribution, at relatively small cost to the Community budget, and thus reduce somewhat the total required.

A much larger budget would, however, still be required, but this need not increase total public expenditure at all levels to the extent that it resulted from a transfer of functions from national governments to the Community; and insofar as favourably placed countries or regions paid more to the Community under redistributive schemes, they might, in the *communautaire* climate assumed for a sustainable EMU, be prepared to cut back somewhat at least the *growth* of their public spending on things other than help to less favoured areas. It sometimes seems strange to me, if countries have the political will to have a single currency, a European Central Bank, with national central banks no more than its operational arms, having no autonomous monetary policy powers, and with the Community having authority over the financing of national budgets, that they do not also have a political will, and feeling of unity, as strong as that in existing economic and monetary unions, and so a readiness to have as powerful equalizing and equilibrating mechanisms as they have.

References
1. As measured by the Gini coefficient.
2. The idea of a Community Unemployment Fund was first proposed in the 'Marjolin' Report of the Study Group (of which I was a member) on 'Economic and Monetary Union 1980', Brussels, March 1975. The Fund would pay a flat money amount per day per unemployed person to national unemployment schemes which could, within certain constraints, remain quite different in accordance with national economic conditions and preferences. The payments would be financed by a uniform percentage levy on wages and salaries. Part of the contributions of individuals in work would be shown as being paid to the Community and part of the receipts of the unemployed as coming from the Community. Apart from the political attractions of bringing individual citizens into direct contact with the Community, the scheme would have significant redistributive effects between richer and poorer countries and between countries with lower and higher unemployment. It would also help to cushion temporary setbacks in particular member countries. Experience in the United States, where the proceeds of a Federal payroll tax — of a uniform percentage of wages, up to a fixed ceiling — were largely paid into State unemployment trust funds, suggested that a strong harmonization of member state schemes would not necessarily be a prerequisite of Community participation. (See pages 389 and 493 of Volume II of the 'MacDougall Report'.)
3. The country would no longer have the power to stimulate domestic demand through lower interest rates; and its power to do so through fiscal policy would be limited by, among other things, the Maastricht rules on government borrowing, or by inability to borrow more than a certain amount on the markets on acceptable terms, or by unwillingness to impose further burdens on future taxpayers.
4. Committee for the Study of Economic and Monetary Union. Report on economic and monetary policy in the Community, 1989.
5. Page 16.
6. See articles by Edward Balls and Martin Wolf in *The Financial Times*, 20 January

and 24 February 1992.

7. As measured by hourly earnings in manufacturing (see MacDougall, *The World Dollar Problem*, 1957, page 82); and the same is broadly true of wage costs per unit of output because productivity in manufacturing rose only marginally faster in the United States.

8. Pages 18 and 13.

9. Luxembourg: Office for Official Publications of the European Communities, 1991. The main authors, Iain Begg and David Mayes, have drawn on the report in their article on 'Social and economic cohesion among the regions of Europe in the 1990s', published in the *National Institute Economic Review*, November 1991.

This article was first published in the Economic Review, *May 1992, of the National Institute for Economic and Social Research.*

CHAPTER 7

Funding the Recovery Programme

Andrew Marvell

The next phase in the development of the case for a European economic recovery programme concerns how to find the money to finance it. On the surface, this should not pose any problems. There is plenty of money available on international capital markets, witnessed in the great speculative fever leading to Black Wednesday. Interest rates, looked at in three to five year terms, are not insuperably expensive, if the money raised by governments can be copper-bottomed for investors. This is something which is not especially difficult, given the variety of paper instruments available in international capital markets.

Nor are the sums of money needed for a sustained recovery programme particularly large. Ken Coates' draft European recovery programme estimates a Community budget in 2012 of between 100 billion ECU and 120 billion ECU for structural funds and external action. Half way along that road, in 1997, this would mean between 35 and 55 billion ECU, and between 62 billion and 80 billion in 2001. At a parity of about 81 pence, the ECU produces Sterling figures for 1997 of £29 billion to £45 billion.

The programme assumes that this is all possible by a fairly straightforward expansion of the EC budget, while at the same time arguing that the current recessionary crisis — it may be more, in the sense that even a modest technical recovery in growth will be on a low growth trend — is less a financial, and more a social and economic crisis. Hence the case for a dramatically accelerated monetary union, as the prerequisite for a major EC budgetary expansion.

This note tries to make the first phase of funding more concrete, and to address a political credibility problem about the case for raising large European funds now, amidst financial instability, inflationary fears in Germany and, by extension, in world recovery perceptions. It recognizes that value added tax cannot be increased dramatically in the member states, at least in the near future, and that public sector borrowing requirement sources of funding are severely limited. It further recognizes the need to address the detailed picture emerging from forecasters of a short-term, largely technical economic recovery in the next eighteen months — partly fuelled by President Clinton's victory in the United States. It may also help to guide us through the maze of economic news, much of it bad. The EC Budget is being lowered because of a downward revision of growth forecasts. The US Federal Reserve chairman, Alan Greenspan, warns that economic forecasting is in no-mans-land, because no one has experienced forecasting with such a major downward asset price trend since 1945, and that the US and Japan could be in for a really long, deep downturn. Japan stands ready to boost further its July 1992 package of £54 billion, because recession carries on, fuelled by bank and land value problems.

My argument is that a prudent, even conservative, mechanism is needed to get the first phase of Euro-funding off the ground. It will not be done by member states — given the current and foreseeable political line-up — granting new powers to the Commission, or any other new body, or even by an accelerated-timetable European bank.

Without mass pressure and extensive political agitation, which would be a tonic for the system's frightened and directionless politicians, the left needs a practical proposal to top out the uplift of its strategic thinking about a new phase of social cohesion in Europe.

And conservativeness of mood is certainly there, not least in some quarters of the labour movement. I think it needs to be both respected and addressed, and I am reminded, amid the clamours of new-found Keynesians, of the undertow of fear in already fearful economic circumstances. I'm sure Ernie Bevin was playing to an audience with his observation about Mr Keynes' money, after a session on the Macmillan Committee, to the effect that somehow it doesn't feel very real in your pocket. 'When I listen to Lord Keynes talking', Bevin said, 'I seem to hear those coins jingling in my pocket, but I am not sure they are really there'. Maybe it was playing to an audience, but we might learn something from that subtle art. Conservativeness in our own ranks means we can't just say 'print lots of money', or 'borrow big now and pay through the nose later'. But I stress that what we have to avoid is making it seem too simple, even if in a rational sense it may well be simple to borrow big and print money later.

What may be possible, however, is to build on the experience of the Exchange Rate Mechanism emergency funding programmes which, we now know, came into place to assist, sometimes too late, sometimes successfully, the weaker European Community currencies around the Black Wednesday period.

The Coates programme combines big scale funding in the crucial short/medium-term future, with low inflationary signals, and economic and monetary union by practical delivery rather than the mauled Treaty programme. It also combines political credibility in the sense that some of the technical co-operation required, and familiarity with the sort of sums required, was forged — albeit in confusion, panic, and amidst mutual recriminations — during the speculative crisis in September 1992. There is also the plain political fact that, without a major general election due, programmes for recovery need to be posed in terms which are difficult to dodge for politicians in power.

A major European bond issue

Consideration should be given to a five year European Recovery Bond issue. This should be demanded from European Finance Ministers, meeting in Ecofin, to be managed by the European Monetary Institute (EMI) once Maastricht has got through. It should seek to raise a credible sum, which also fits in with formal economic forecasts, and should be presented in terms that address the serious collective unemployment problem of the Community, such that there is foreseeable collective gain to public finances from the work creation aspect of the European Economic Recovery Programme Bond issue.

This is a key requirement. For, as the Coates' figures show, any modest, "natural" upturn in Europe is likely to leave structural unemployment high. As it is competition driven, it will raise productivity, and make unemployment relatively worse. It is an economic problem which the driver of a car with a faulty gearbox might readily understand. Driving in bottom and second gear at least keeps you moving forward, but the weight of the unemployed passengers means that moving to third gear is very difficult and, if achieved, will probably slow you down, even if, to reflect the current decline in some interest rates, petrol consumption drops a bit. The name of the game is to get into top gear to lighten the load, and really benefit from fuel economy.

The bond issue should be backed by an agreed percentage of all 12 countries' central bank reserves, which should be set aside in an ecu pool to back the ecu denominated issue. The size could be of the minimum order of £150 billion sterling, giving annual structural funds and external action funds of the order of £30 billion.

Of course, much of the reserve of foreign currencies and gold and International Monetary Fund drawing rights held by the diversely organized central banks of the 12, are simply paper balances. But, if Economic and Monetary Union is to proceed, this amount of paper will not be required, so the promise — and the political signal to speculative forces — of some of these reserves being pooled to redeem the bond issue would allow it to be offered to the market on attractive terms. For instance, although denominated in ecu, it could be paid back in currencies of investors' choice, subject to the requirement that this option be notified at a decent interval of, say, six months. If the EMU integration progress were sufficient by then, and the medicine had worked, the ecu might be an attractive currency in its own right. That is a political speculation itself, of course, but the message should be plain: there is an urgent need to look for funding instruments which contain the seeds of monetary and economic cohesion within them.

Reserves

The arithmetic of using a tranche of the reserves of the 12 to underpin the bond issue is quite straightforward. Britain's £7 billion emergency reserves were piled on top of about £44 billion existing reserves. The 12 have reserves of about £170 billion, and, under a formally achieved EMU with a European Bank, would not need anything like this amount. Japan has total currency reserves of only £44 billion, and the USA £40 billion.

If, say, a third or a half of the recovery bond issue were to be funded by some book-keeping on the reserves, the real burden of servicing it would be less onerous. There might be takers at slightly lower than market interest rate, simply because the combined effects of using some reserves, and the growth outturn's effects on public borrowing, would promise reasonable prospects of a non-inflationary recovery.

It has been objected that this sort of approach would give powers and responsibilities to central bankers who are neither equipped to exercise it, nor likely to have any political sympathy with the objectives. It is a useful clarificatory point, but the only role I see for the central banks and the European Monetary Institute is to carry out political instructions to raise the money, which would need to be deposited into a special recovery fund, on top of the existing European Community budget. That is, there is a lot of work to be done on practical political and institutional mechanisms for controlling sums of money of this order. Not the least interesting might be a key role for the European Parliament. And could there even be a case for a supplement to Maastricht, to add a chapter on economic recovery to the Treaty, rather than to attempt to incorporate verbal morsels to appease the unclear discontents of the Danes, the whole process simply leaving the unemployed swimming around in a sea of potentially dangerous political diversions?

Spending

How might the money be spent? If the bond issue was drip-fed over six months to a year, expenditure could be released in quarterly blocks on the basis of, say, half for public sector works/investment relief in each country, and half of the total for European level agreed programmes of infrastructure development. Country level action could be immediate, and European programmes could start in, say, six months. The latter would start a debate about which existing administered European Community programmes could be expanded rapidly, thus establishing a Keynesian intervention dimension to some European Community budget heads, which are currently purely structural and fiscally neutral in the short term.

On the "politics", there are two levels. Firstly, overcoming public suspicion about European federalism, which this scheme implements, both by taking action in advance of Treaties/ institutions as a practical programme, and also by adding to the Treaty a dimension — the Recovery Chapter — which should have been in it to start with. Secondly, the left requires its own profile, aside from having pressed for, and won, a new phenomenon — a European scale U-turn.

The left might consider some urgent demands for the halting of some European Community programmes which, in deep recession, will be unemployment creating, even if, in expansionary circum-stances, they might have been marginal net job creators. The public sector deregulation measures being pursued by the European Community might be frozen for two years, so that the existing public sector spending mechanisms can be quickly used to disburse some of the ecu Bond issue, in rail, roads, and a European cable network, some boosted research and development areas, and so on.

Getting capitalist investment going requires specific mechanisms. So, at traded sector, real economy level, could not European level/size companies, using the draft Directive on an emergency, temporary basis, be invited to borrow from the Bond fund in return for agreed accelerated investment tax breaks, which would also be part of the pragmatic package. The draft Directive could be agreed summarily, for a two to three year period, by the Parliament and the Council under co-decision terms. The French would love it, because of their semi-state firms under pressure from Britain, and, behind the scenes, with British Aerospace going downish, even Mr Major might be interested.

CHAPTER 8

Planning the Recovery Programme

Stuart Holland

A European recovery programme is imperative if Europe is not to face grave social tensions in the 1990's.

If there is no significant change in Community expenditure, nor an active macroeconomic policy, nor major changes in favour of economic and social cohesion, the results will be disastrous for employment and income. On the basis of figures from Alphametrics Cambridge, unemployment in Spain and Ireland could be at 25 per cent within ten years; there could be 15 per cent unemployment in Italy and 12.5 per cent in France.

This is a scenario of the unacceptable. Such figures do not take account of disguised unemployment or under-employment in individual countries. In this respect they are an under-statement rather than over-statement. Besides this, the situation in parts of central and eastern Europe is unstable. The breakdown of Yugoslavia has already meant that up to two-thirds of a million refugees are pressing for access or asylum in the Community. A disaster scenario is possible in the republics of the Commonwealth of Independent States.

In such a context it is not only Maastricht that will not hold. In some countries, democracy itself will be discredited if governments do not act to promote recovery through policies for both internal and external cohesion.

The dilemma is that Maastricht worsens the prospect of national recovery through the deflation that would be needed to meet the 3 per cent deficit limits. Further borrowing is ruled out for some countries because they also exceed the Maastricht limits on national debt.

Cohesion policies within the Community are not likely to gain major additions to own resources (the Community's budget) during the next five years in which the demands of environmental protection and economic and social support for the reforming economies are so pressing.

On the other hand, neither internal cohesion nor monetary union will be possible in the Community by the later 1990's unless policies are pursued that promote not only financial, but also economic and social convergence.

In practice the budget deficit conditions of Maastricht may not be met. But their criteria relate to an earlier era, before the implications of the massive needs of German reunification or the reforming economies were fully grasped.

Recovery plus

The Community needs to achieve more than a Keynesian recovery programme. If new policies are not adopted for internal cohesion, the reduction of budget deficits will both aggravate internal tensions and contract intra-Community trade. The resulting unemployment could be worse than those in the base scenario figures.

However, a key reason why recovery has to be Keynes-Plus is that increased spending alone will not create enough new jobs, since, with technical progress, much new investment now displaces labour.

Also, much of the social cohesion that was feasible in the third of a century after the war, through growth and social mobility, now needs to be consciously achieved through a range of policies that then were not necessary.

For these reasons the strategy for recovery cannot simply be increased expenditure. The Community needs to:

- recover spending, trade and employment,
- restructure firms, industries and regions,
- reinforce rights for women, rights at work, and civil rights for minorities;
- reduce annual working hours in bigger business and the public sector;
- redistribute resources to specific economic and social needs.

Exempting agreed social programmes

None the less, a recovery programme and the macroeconomic context are crucial to the outcome. Otherwise, the issue is not simply whether some countries will integrate their currencies, but whether the Community itself will disintegrate under conflicting claims on resources and increased unwillingness to support income transfers. The key issue is how to fund recovery granted the national budget deficit limits in Maastricht.

One means would be to exempt items of social expenditure necessary for cohesion from the national budget deficit limits. Capital expenditure projects on education and training, health, and social provision should come into this category. They should be exempted from the Maastricht limits on national budgets and transferred to the Community budget.

The Delors 2 package of February 1992 made explicit reference to the need to consider cohesion expenditures not simply in terms of infrastructure or regional development, but also their possible extension to social spending. Possibly this recommendation will be reinforced in the new two year programme this autumn, on which the President gave a commitment to the European Parliament on the vote of approval of the new Commission in February.

Such exemptions, none the less, would need another inter-governmental conference (IGC) to provide a protocol amending the national budgetary and borrowing conditions in this regard. Again, this need not be wholly intimidating. IGC's take place all the time without the hullabaloo of Maastricht. If governments are serious on the matter — because of loss of political support with national austerity — they could fix such a protocol within a few months.

However, it is more likely that such a provision would be duly processed and ratified by governments towards the end of the Delors two year programme, as should reinforcement of economic and civil rights with a strengthened Social Charter for, at least, its original signatories.

The European Investment Fund

A key potential breakthrough on how to finance recovery and cohesion has been achieved by the decision of the Edinburgh Summit to establish a borrowing and spending agency in the form of the European Investment Fund (EIF). Proposed to the Commission last year within the context of the above arguments, its statutes had not yet been drafted by mid-January 1993. However, it has potential as an instrument for Keynesian expenditure policies.

First, it will be administered not by a committee of governors of central banks but by the European Investment Bank (EIB). Second, its expenditure will not be determined by the EIB but by the Community. This is already indicated by the Commission proposal that its initial terms of reference will be to finance (i) the transeuropean networks of transport infrastructure projects specified in Maastricht and (ii) small and medium-sized firms. Third, the EIF will have significant multiplier effects over and above its own resources, like the principle of the 'counterpart funds' of the initial Marshall Aid programme administered by the Organization for European Economic Co-operation (OEEC).

The multipliers will reinforce the leverage of the Fund's lending. The estimates from the Commission are that while the total subscribed capital of the Fund will in the first instance amount to only 2 billion ECU, this will be able to extend guarantees on lending of up to 10 billion ECU, which in total could support up to 20 billion ECU worth of projects. The latter figure implies that governments or firms will be able to match lending from the Fund for projects which they otherwise would not have undertaken only on their own resources.

Several points need to be stressed.

(1) the Fund will borrow from both the European Investment Bank and also from other financial institutions;

(2) it will therefore in practice operate as the Community equivalent of a collective national debt;

(3) the rate of interest it needs to return on its borrowings should be lower than those of any individual member states because it will be determined in the ecu basket of currencies, thereby offsetting the risk of devaluation of one or more national currencies.

In effect, there is major potential in the new European Investment Fund. None the less, it still is potential rather than actual. Its actual terms of reference and statutes have yet to be ratified at the forthcoming European Council meeting in June.

Further, its resources and terms of reference need to be increased to make the contribution to European recovery for which it is designed. In practice it should be boosting expenditures by up to 20 or 30 billion ecu each year rather than over a four year period, as at present envisaged.

In this context, and granted the worsening of the recession in the Community even since December 1992, when the EIF was agreed in principle at the Edinburgh Summit, the June 1993 European Council should:

● urge an acceleration of the programmes of the EIF so that they can begin as soon as possible this year;

● agree the proposed terms of reference on the Fund on lending to finance transeuropean networks and small and medium-sized firms;

● include lending to areas of environmental protection and energy production — already anticipated by the proposal of the Commission on the Fund for a later stage of its activities;

● explicitly extend its terms of reference to include overhead social capital such as investment in housing, urban and regional renewal, and general economic and social infrastructure;[1]

● ensure that its remit in terms of areas of expenditure is open-ended and thereby can include whatever expenditure is deemed necessary by the Council on a majority vote to ensure its declared aims of promoting both economic recovery and economic and social cohesion.

The Bundesbank and the European Central Bank

The creation of the new European Investment Fund makes it credible to meet one of the main objections to Maastricht: that is, that an independent European Central Bank — like the Bundesbank — would be able to block recovery.

There is widespread misunderstanding both about the powers of the Bundesbank and the powers of the proposed ECB. There are real fears that the independence of the ECB on the Bundesbank model would mean that an appointed and unremovable committee of governors would be able to give priority to monetary stability in such a manner as to deny Community governments the right to pursue a recovery programme under recessionary conditions. Such independence — if true — would amount to Euromonetarism, and should be rejected.

But fears are not facts. In practice the independence or autonomy or the Bundesbank is relative. The same goes in Maastricht for what would be the European Central Bank.

The political constraints on the Bundesbank are evident in what happened to the Deutschmark on German reunification. It is common knowledge that the Bundesbank was wholly opposed to parity for the Ostmark and the Deutschmark. In practice, it was overruled by Chancellor Kohl. Various views can be expressed on the merits of the Bundesbank's case for a gradual alignment of the value of the Deutschmark and the Ostmark. It is strongly arguable that both the Bundesbank and Oskar Lafontaine — then leader of the SPD — were right to argue that currency alignment and the transition costs of unification should be phased.

Many comments were made at the time that Chancellor Kohl bounced the Bundesbank against its better advice. So how did he do it if the Bundesbank were indeed "independent of government"? For one thing he was helped by a key element in the terms of reference of the Bundesbank. Article 3 of the constitution of the bank requires it to defend the internal and external value of the currency. But a provision attached to article 12 also obliges it explicitly "to support the general economic policy aims of the federal government".

Put differently, there is a "dual power" provision in the terms of reference of the Bundesbank. The duality is between bankers and politicians. And in the case of German unification, the politicians won. Chancellor Kohl did not simply "bounce the bank"; he had the constitutional right to do so.

Likewise, when Philippe Seguin claimed to François Mitterrand in their televised debate before the French referendum that Maastricht would give independence on monetary policy to the ECB, Mitterrand rebutted this, claiming that the European Council of heads of state and heads of government would be free to determine the general economic policies of the Community, and that the ECB would be obliged to support this.

The following morning most of the French press claimed that the old survivor was out of touch and that Seguin had a better feel for Maastricht. This only shows that many journalists, like at least one British Cabinet minister, simply have not read the Treaty. They were wrong. In claiming that the European Council had the final say, President Mitterrand was as right for the Community as was Chancellor Kohl in terms of parity for the Deutschmark and Ostmark on German reunification.

The writ is there in the Maastricht Treaty, where article 105 provides two main terms of reference for the ECB. They are (1) that "the primary objective of the ECB shall be to maintain price stability" and (2) that "without prejudice to the objective of price stability, the ECB shall support the general economic policies in the Community with a view to contributing to the achievement of the objectives of the Community as laid down in article 2".

Article 2 of Maastricht is crucial. It is far more explicit than the obligation of the Bundesbank in its own constitution. It specifies that:

> the Community shall have as its task, by establishing a common market and an economic and monetary union and by implementing the common policies referred to in Article 3 and 3a, to promote throughout the Community a harmonious and balanced development of economic activities, sustainable and non-inflationary growth respecting the environment, a high degree of convergence of economic performance, a high level of employment and of social protection, the raising of the standard of living and the quality of life, and economic and social cohesion and solidarity among Member States.

Article 3 summarizes the broad range of Comunity policies. Article 3a(1) specifies that, for the purposes set out in article 2,

> the activities of the Member States and the Community shall include . . . the adoption of an economic policy which is based on the close coordination of Member States' economic policies, of the internal market and on the definition of common objectives.

Much of Maastricht is incomprehensible, drafted in a rush to meet summit deadlines. No doubt this is why some politicians and journalists misrepresent them. But these articles concerning the powers of the ECB were well drafted. They also are in an active political mode. The ECB is not simply obliged to pursue monetary policy consistent with the "general economic policies of the Community" but to "contribute to the achievement of the objectives". The objectives do not simply include price stability or monetary union but also a high degree of economic convergence, a high level of employment and social protection, and the raising of the standard of living.

Such an agenda should be welcome in Britain. Besides, if Maastricht were a formula for Euro-monetarism, why should the rumour be so widespread that key figures in the Bundesbank do not support it? Why indeed should Margaret Thatcher not support it? Such a Treaty would have enshrined her more forcefully in European history than the re-entombment of Jean Monnet in Les Invalides.

The answer lies in the above provisions and the political space which they give for governments to pursue other objectives than priority for monetary stability. The obligation on the ECB to contribute to the achievement of balanced development, sustainable growth, respect for the environment, a high level of employment and social protection, and the raising of the standard of living and quality of life are explicit expression of the demand which Jacques Delors has made that monetary union should respect the objectives of economic and social cohesion. He did this when he took over the presidency of the committee of governors of central banks to draft the report on monetary union in his name, in which such commitment is explicit.

Likewise it is too often overlooked that cohesion is a parallel objective of the internal market programme as specified in the Single European Act.

Moreover, Maastricht spells out other provisions which are anathema to Thatcherism, including (i) the commitment to a European industrial strategy; (ii) the right of the European TUC and European Employers' Federation to initiate Community policy on improved labour relations and social provisions for labour, and (iii) the provision for a Committee of the Regions that should enable local authorities in the United Kingdom to gain political and economic leverage irrespective of the abolition of regional authorities by a centralizing Tory administration.

Clearly the industrial strategy provisions in Maastricht need strengthening in practice. But the potential for this is there, especially through the process of the Social Dialogue, which itself reverses the long criticised practice whereby it is only the Commission which can propose initiatives, and the Council of Ministers recommend amendments.

The German question

One of the main confusions around Maastricht is between monetary policy as a means of indirect influence on money supply, and government economic policy in the sphere of public borrowing and expenditure.

Clearly high interest rates will affect the cost of government borrowing or borrowing by the new European Investent Fund. But they cannot stop such borrowing if governments are determined. Besides which, as stressed above, the new EIF should be able to set interest rates that are lower than the Community average by virtue of its borrowing in ecu, which thereby spreads the risk of realignment of any one of them.

Those who claim that the European Central Bank would simply be dominated by the Bundesbank should recognize that the Bundesbank, in fact, has set low real rates for long periods of high economic growth. It is not simply a monetarist disposition within the bank, but German reunification that caused the very high recent real rates from the bank. The terms of reunification not only showed the limits to the power of the Bundesbank. It also has weakened Germany itself.

However, with the costs and problems of reunification, German attitudes to issues such as industrial, social and regional policy have changed. And this is important for such policies at Community level in the 1990s.

In the Federal Republic, during the period of the *Wirtschaftswunder*, the structural, social and regional balance in the economy was exceptional by the standards of any other European economy. This was partly historical in the sense that the capitals of the Lander still retained their autonomous character as centres of business and culture, established over centuries before the emergence of a unified state in 1871. Some of the most modern industry in Germany was moved to the South to avoid allied bombing. Much of it now is threatened severely by Japanese competition, such as the motor industries of Baden Wurttemberg and Bavaria, which could well follow the fate of the West Midlands within the next few years unless the Social Dialogue and industrial policy provisions of Maastricht are implemented.

But, besides this, interregional balance in Germany has changed dramatically with the task of absorbing the Lander of the former GDR. Germany now is faced with structural, social, regional and environmental problems on a scale without precedent in any other Community country.

This, rather than the formal powers of the Bundesbank, is the key reason why German interest rates are so high and why they are imposing a penal cost on the rest of Europe. The way out is not to keep knocking the Bundesbank and the Bonn government but to take seriously the potential of the new European Investment Fund as the public expenditure means outside Maastricht that can take the strain of the federal German budget and thereby make possible a lowering of German interest rates.

Much of this reasoning lay behind the call of Jacques Delors and the Commission before Edinburgh for a European Recovery Programme, and the decision at Edinburgh to establish the European Investment Fund. It is a call that, with the demand for new industrial, social and regional policies in Maastricht, progressive forces in Britain should join and support.

Medium term planning

Besides which, as the better of Margaret Thatcher's former or actual advisers should have alerted her, Maastricht actually spells out the means by which the "general economic policies" to whose achievement the ECB is bound to contribute, can be determined by majority vote on the Council of Ministers (article 103.2).

Thus no one country such as the UK can block a recovery programme. Further, the relevant institutions already are in place.

The anonymous Economic Policy Committee in Maastricht is composed of national representatives. They already can forward proposals for the "general economic policies" embodied in article 105 on the responsibilities of the ECB, and forward them to the Committee of Finance Ministers (ECOFIN) for recommendation to the European Council.

This Economic Policy Committee is the successor of the Medium Term Economic Policy Committee established by Robert Marjolin as Vice President of the Commission in 1964. Marjolin was a planner who learned the need to intervene from none other than Jean Monnet when he was the highly interventionist head of the First French Plan. When made head of OEEC, in 1948, Marjolin had been instrumental in sending back national shopping lists for reconstruction, and insisting that countries had to draw up a medium term plan in which it would be evident in what way choices were made, and how decisions on allocation affected both the economy and society as a whole. The first report of the Medium Term Economic Policy Committee, in March 1966, set out a planning exercise for the Community by which macroeconomic targets for employment and income were matched by industrial, social and regional policy objectives. It was this, at the time, which persuaded Harold Wilson that membership of the Community was compatible with the 1965 National Plan.

The role of Marjolin's committee was downgraded following the impact of the 1973 oil shock, that is, at the time when most governments lost faith in their capacity to undertake joint international planning or programming.

However, one of the main indirect effects of the deflationary national provisions in Maastricht has been to increase the pressure from the European Parliament for not only recovery, but also recovery with a strategy for the medium term. Notably, Jacques Delors stressed the importance not only of recovery but also of a medium term strategy to achieve it in his address to the Socialist Group of the European Parliament in February 1993.

Democracy and planning

The Community should not only set general economic objectives through the European Council as required by article 3a(1) of Maastricht. It also should do so on a basis that widens both debate and pressure on alternative allocations of the resources themselves.

There are five related imperatives for both coherent economic policy and for cohesion:

(1) that the commitment should be political, and perceived as such by most member governments, by Community institutions, and outside them in the Community as a whole;

(2) that the Committee should restore the commitment of Marjolin's MTEPC to the formulation of a medium term economic policy programme for the Community;[2]

(3) that the medium-term programme should be rolled forward on an annual basis in such a way that it can take account of change in the internal or external economic and financial environment;

(4) that the Committee should both present macroeconomic scenarios and their structural, social and spatial dimensions in the manner pioneered by the Marjolin committee;

(5) that the debate on general economic policies should be democratized, which should coincide with an agreed six months of the calendar year.

The case for a six monthly cycle within a calendar year is simply practical. In the UK the budget is presented in the spring but then debated in committee in the form of a Finance Bill, with a further "autumn statement".

The point is precisely that the general economic policies of the Community, unlike the short-term interest rate decisions that may be undertaken by the European Central Bank, can be fully and properly debated by the relevant parliaments on an on-going basis for at least half the calendar cycle.

In such a way the main strategic options before the Community on the rate of economic growth, the level of employment and its distribution between sectors, social groups and regions would become part of the on-going debate in not only Community institutions but also the relevant national and regional media. In turn, such a debate would give rise to pressures on and from elected representatives that would reinforce democratization of the Community itself.

Such a process would improve on the Commission exercise of forecasting the use of only its own budget, because the scenarios to be considered would include alternative strategies for the economies of the member states as well as common policies. Such alternatives should include different combinations of spending on economic, social and regional policies within different macroeconomic options.

This would vastly improve on the Westminster practice of (i) debating the Commission's budget rather than the future of the European economy, (ii) doing so months after the budget has been decided by the Council, and (iii) thereby failing even to recommend changes or amendments.

It would bring democratic choice into the heart of the economic and social project for Europe, demonstrating the feasibility of a Community for people rather than a Community seemingly concerned only with markets and money.

References
1. The category of general infrastructure should be evident, and allow member states to implement a wide range of projects that have been suspended because of the deflationary terms of Maastricht on public expenditure. The category of social infrastructure could and should include investment in facilities for education, training, and retraining, as well as the Innovation Centres proposed in the context of regional development.
2. This was dropped in practice by the metamorphosis of the MTEPC into the General Economic Policy Committee.

CHAPTER 9

A Federal Government?

Wynne Godley

A lot of people throughout Europe have suddenly realized that they know hardly anything about the Maastricht Treaty, while rightly sensing that it could make a huge difference to their lives. Their legitimate anxiety has provoked Jacques Delors to make a statement to the effect that the views of ordinary people should, in future, be more sensitively consulted. He might have thought of that before.

Although I support the move towards political integration in Europe, I think that the Maastricht proposals as they stand are seriously defective, and also that public discussion of them has been curiously impoverished. With a Danish rejection, a near-miss in France, and the very existence of the Exchange Rate Mechanism in question after the depredations by currency markets, it is a good moment to take stock.

The central idea of the Maastricht Treaty is that the European Community countries should move towards an economic and monetary union, with a single currency, managed by a central bank. But how is the rest of economic policy to be run? As the treaty proposes no new institutions other than a European bank, its sponsors must suppose that nothing more is needed. But this could only be correct if modern economies were self-adjusting systems that didn't need any management at all.

I am driven to the conclusion that such a view — that economies are self-righting organisms which never, under any circumstances, need management at all — did indeed determine the way in which the Maastricht Treaty was framed. It is a crude and extreme version of the view which, for some time now, has constituted Europe's conventional wisdom (though not that of the US or Japan) that governments are unable, and therefore should not try, to achieve any of the traditional goals of economic policy, such as growth and full employment. All that can legitimately be done, according to this view, is to control the money supply and balance the budget. It took a group, largely composed of bankers (the Delors Committee), to reach the conclusion that an independent central bank was the only supra-national institution necessary to run an integrated, supra-national Europe.

But there is much more to it all. It needs to be emphasized at the start that the establishment of a single currency in the European Community would indeed bring to an end the sovereignty of its component nations, and their power to take independent action on major issues. As Mr Tim Congdon has argued very cogently, the power to issue its own money, to make drafts on its own central bank, is the main thing which defines national independence. If a country gives up or loses this power, it acquires the status of a local authority, or colony. Local authorities and regions obviously cannot devalue. But they also lose the power to finance deficits through money creation, while other methods of raising finance are subject to central regulation. Nor can they change interest rates. As local authorities possess none of the instruments of macro-economic policy, their political choice is confined to relatively minor matters of emphasis — a bit more education here, a bit less infrastructure there. I think that when Jacques Delors lays new emphasis on the principle of 'subsidiarity', he is really only telling us we will be allowed to make decisions about a larger number of relatively unimportant matters than we might previously have supposed. Perhaps he will let us have curly cucumbers after all. Big deal!

A different view

Let me express a different view. I think that the central government of any sovereign state ought to be striving all the time to determine the optimum overall level of public provision, the correct overall burden of taxation, the correct allocation of total expenditures between competing requirements, and the just distribution of the tax burden. It must also determine the extent to which any gap between expenditure and taxation is financed by making a draft on the central bank, and how much it is financed by borrowing, and on what terms. The way in which the governments decide all these (and some other) issues, and the quality of leadership which they can deploy, will, in interaction with the decisions of individuals, corporations and foreigners, determine such things as interest rates, the exchange rate, the inflation rate, the growth rate, and the unemployment rate. It will also profoundly influence the distribution of income and wealth, not only between individuals, but between whole regions, assisting, one hopes, those adversely affected by structural change.

Almost nothing simple can be said about the use of these instruments, with all their interdependencies, to promote the well-being of a nation, and protect it as well as may be from the shocks of various kinds to which it will inevitably be subjected. It only has limited meaning. For instance, to say that budgets should always be balanced, when a balanced budget with expenditure and taxation running at 40 per cent of Gross Domestic Product would have an entirely different (and much more expansionary) impact than a balanced budget at 10 per cent of GDP. To imagine the complexity and importance of a government's macro-economic decisions, one has only to ask what would be the appropriate response, in terms of fiscal, monetary, and exchange rate policy for a country about to produce large quantities of oil, of a four-fold increase in the price of oil. Would it have been right to do nothing at all? And it should never be forgotten that, in periods of very great crisis, it may even be appropriate for a central government to sin against the Holy Ghost of all central banks, and invoke the 'inflation tax' — deliberately appropriating resources by reducing, through inflation, the real value of a nation's paper wealth.

I recite all this to suggest, not that sovereignty should not be given up in the noble cause of European integration, but that if all these functions are renounced by individual governments, they simply have to be taken on by some other authority. The incredible lacuna in the Maastricht programme is that, while it contains a blueprint for the establishment and *modus operandi* of an independent central bank, there is no blueprint whatever of the analogue, in Community terms, of a central government. Yet there would simply have to be a system of institutions which fulfils all those functions at a Community level, which are, at present, exercised by the central governments of individual member countries.

The counterpart of giving up sovereignty should be that the component nations are constituted into a federation to whom their sovereignty is entrusted. And the federal system, or government, as it had better be called, would have to exercise all those functions in relation to its members and to the outside world that I have briefly outlined above.

Co-ordinated action

Consider two important examples of what a federal government, in charge of a federal budget, should be doing.

European countries are at present locked into a severe recession. As things stand, particularly as the economies of the USA and Japan are also faltering, it is very unclear when any significant recovery will take place. The political implications of this are becoming frightening. Yet the inter-dependence of the European economies is already so great that no individual country, with the theoretical exception of Germany, feels able to pursue expansionary policies on its own, because any country that did try to expand on its own would soon encounter a balance of payments constraint. The present situation is screaming aloud for co-ordinated reflation, but there exist neither the institutions, nor an agreed framework of thought which will bring about this obviously desirable result. It should be frankly recognized that, if the depression really were to take a serious turn for the worse — for instance, if the unemployment rate went back permanently to the 20-25 per cent characteristic of the Thirties — individual countries would sooner or later exercise their sovereign right to declare the entire movement towards integration a disaster, and resort to exchange controls and protection — a siege economy, if you will. This would amount to a re-run of the inter-war period.

If there were an economic and monetary union, in which the power to act independently had actually been abolished, co-ordinated reflation of the kind which is so urgently needed now, could only be undertaken by a federal European government. Without such an institution, European Monetary Union would prevent effective action by individual countries, and put nothing in its place.

Another important role which any central government must perform, is to put a safety net under the livelihood of component regions which are in distress for structural reasons — because of the decline of some industry, say, or because of some economically-adverse demographic change. At present this happens in the natural course of events, without anyone really noticing, because common standards of public provision (for instance, health, education, pensions and rates of employment benefit) and a common (it is to be hoped, progressive) burden of taxation are both generally instituted throughout individual realms. As a consequence, if one region suffers an unusual degree of structural decline, the fiscal system automatically generates net transfers in favour of it. *In extremis*, a region which could produce nothing at all would not starve, because it would be in receipt of pensions, unemployment benefit and the incomes of public servants.

Federal arrangements

What happens if a whole country — a potential 'region' in a fully integrated community — suffers a structural setback? So long as it is a sovereign state, it can devalue its currency. It can trade successfully at full employment provided its people accept the necessary cut in their real incomes. With an economic and monetary union, this recourse is obviously barred, and its prospect is grave indeed, unless federal budgeting arrangements are made that fulfil a redistributive role. As was clearly recognized in the MacDougall Report in 1977, there has to be a *quid pro quo* for giving up the devaluation option in the form of fiscal redistribution.

Some writers (such as Samuel Brittan and Sir Douglas Hague) have seriously suggested that European Monetary Union, by abolishing the balance of payments problem in its present form, would indeed abolish the problem, where it exists, of persistent failure to compete successfully in world markets. But, as Professor Martin Feldstein pointed out in a major article in the *Economist* (13th June 1992), this argument is very dangerously mistaken. If a country or region has no power to devalue, and it is not the beneficiary of a system of fiscal equalization, then there is nothing to stop it suffering a process of cumulative and terminal decline, leading, in the end, to emigration as the only alternative to poverty or starvation. I sympathize with the position of those (like Margaret Thatcher) who, faced with the loss of sovereignty, wish to get off the European Monetary Union train altogether. I also sympathize with those who seek integration under the jurisdiction of some kind of federal constitution with a federal budget very much larger than that of the Community budget. What I find totally baffling is the position of those who are aiming for economic and monetary union without the creation of new political institutions (apart from a new central bank), and who raise their hands in horror at the words 'federal' or 'federalism'. This is the position currently adopted by the Government, and by most of those who take part in the public discussion.

CHAPTER 10

Hard Times

What hopes for European social policy?

Peter Townsend

Despite economic growth in recent decades, people in Britain are glumly aware that the nation's social problems have deepened. This is openly acknowledged by the leaders of the different churches no less than by social scientists. There are beggars in the streets and people sleeping rough in many of the small towns, and not only the metropolitan cities, of Britain. Rates of theft and of imprisonment, and suicides of young people in prison, are of national concern. Race relations in inner cities are tense and, in places like Tower Hamlets, spill over too often into violence. By any of the conventional criteria we care to take, long-term unemployment is widespread and poverty more pervasive than it was.

Poverty in Britain

There are grounds for believing that many of the problems increased rapidly under the Thatcher Government. But it would be wrong not to acknowledge that most have had a longer gestation. The first substantial increase in the post-war unemployment rate (leaving aside the special conditions of the fuel crisis of 1947) was in 1967, and there was a further rise in the rate in the early, and then in the late, 1970s. Or to give a different example, 1976 was the year of the severest cuts in public expenditure. Or again, for decades few in Britain realized how thin were many of its welfare provisions — by comparison, that is, with a large number of European counterparts.

Our predicament is of course in large measure one brought about nationally. There are many studies which demonstrate the relatively greater inequalities of the British class structure, the greater concentrations of wealth at one extreme and of poverty at the other, and the nagging self-destructiveness of deferential attitudes on the part of large numbers in the population, but also overweeningly patronising professional attitudes of many elites. The individualistic rather than collectivistic values built into social and not just economic policies have also contributed to the perpetuation instead of resolution of different classes of citizenship.

In the significant phrase of the mid-1960s, poverty was "rediscovered". Yes, historians would agree that it had been diminished. But, yes, they would also agree it had persisted despite the 1942-1948 reforms, and was certainly larger in scale than was implied by the dismissive word "residual".

What has to be understood is that such poverty was, all along, a product of what can be called "minimalism" — the policy of making sweeping gestures and smallest real concessions to the poor. Minimalism was reflected in the low level of benefits such as family allowances, sickness benefits, and state pensions. It was reflected in the application of means-testing to millions of people in what was the biggest example of the operation of the policies of selective discrimination in Europe, although smaller in coverage than those operating in the United States. Elsewhere I have tried to explain British approaches historically to the welfare state by invoking three models of social policy: (i) conditional welfare for the few; (ii) minimum rights for the many, and (iii) distributional justice for all. Britain was always unusual among European countries in maintaining such strong preference for the first of these three models, and events have sadly reinforced that tradition. None the less, for many years after the 1939 war there remained in Britain considerable complacency about the welfare state on right and left, and widespread disposition on either flank, for different reasons, to exaggerate its scale. We may wryly conclude that the colonial tradition, and especially its invocations of "greatness" or supremacy, helped to maintain not just the illusions of power but also the illusions of welfare.

Redistribution of income and collective provision of public services are now much weaker features of British policy than of the policies of many other European countries. This was true by the mid-1970s, and is not just a phenomenon of the 1980s. Thus, by 1981 social expenditure as a percentage of gross domestic product was significantly less than the average for the 17 member countries of the Organization for Economic Co-operation and Development, and was lowest of the then nine member countries of the European Community. Countries like the Netherlands, Belgium, Denmark and Germany were spending about half as much again on welfare as Britain. Moreover, the differential had been continuing to get bigger. During 1975 to 1981, expenditure on welfare was growing at the second lowest rate among the 17 member countries of the OECD. In fact, it had been the second lowest rate throughout the preceding 15 years as well. Unemployment and sickness benefits and pensions compare poorly with similar benefits in Europe in terms of what goods they will purchase, as well as their low levels relative to earnings.

The latest information from the Statistical Office of the European Communities confirms this trend. In the 1980s, the ranking of different member countries according to their expenditure on what is euphemistically called "Social Protection" (health, housing, social security, family care and community welfare — but not education) has been affected by variations in the years when there has been substantial unemployment, and hence variable expenditure on unemployment benefits. None the less, six member countries, excluding the UK, are in a league with distinctly more generous social provisions than the others, with the United Kingdom, Ireland and Italy in a second, less generous group, and only Greece, Spain and Portugal in the least generous group. The United Kingdom is the only member country which records a fall in expenditure per person between 1985 and 1988 — the latest years for which information exists.

The reluctant Europeans

If the colonial inheritance is one relatively unrecognized influence upon Britain's own social development and policies, Europeanization is another. The British appear to be the reluctant Europeans. They are Europeans primarily because of economic imperatives. They are reluctant because of the stand-offishness induced not only by the imperial tradition but by the traditions of a distinctively class society, and one with strong North American connections.

In one sense, Britain has felt obliged to bow to the inevitable and take the steps necessary to meet her economic self-interests. In the 12 years up to 1969, following the Rome Treaty, real earnings in EEC countries increased by 75 per cent, compared with 40 per cent in Britain. Economic growth was double the British rate, and the rate of investment was much larger. The EEC ran a large balance of payments surplus while the UK ran a deficit. Politicians became concerned to stem the decline, especially in an expanding "Common Market". After two unsuccessful attempts, Britain ratified the Treaty of Accession in 1972. The European Community now has a combined population of nearly 350 millions. That has been the tempting target for preferential market operations, which has helped to overcome some of the scruples of those previously obsessed with national independence.

But, there is a paradox in the behaviour of the present Government. On the one hand, that Government has been responding more swiftly, and more radically, to international market forces than any of its European neighbours. This may explain its objections to the attempts by the majority of the members of the European Community to maintain old-style welfare states during the restructuring of the European economy.

On the other hand, it is promulgating an old-fashioned belief in the independence of the nation state, when such independence is far less viable than ever it was. This may explain its indifference to external causes of new, or deepening, social problems at home, and its ignorance of the need for new strategies and policies which involve European institutions to meet British as well as continental problems. The question is not whether, but how, to live together. Collective values, collective relationships and collective organization have become more necessary just at the time when the Government has been telling us they matter less.

There is a double problem. It is to check likely deterioration in the social conditions of minorities and of the poor simultaneously in Britain and in the rest of Europe. It is going to be an uphill task to develop adequate European social policies or adequate independent national policies in substitution.

The Social Charter

One example of the problem is the debate raging around the Social Charter. In judging the meaning and likely effects of the Social Charter its genesis has to be explained. From the beginning the European Community was what might be called "economistic". The objectives and programmes of the Community were governed by relatively short-term economic values. It has to be seen as an organization seeking to enhance its wealth and its power in relation to the rest of the world. In exchange for the scrapping of national controls like import duties and tariffs among members, prosperity could be guaranteed by extending the internal market to all members of the new club and by confronting countries outside with tougher conditions of trade. The freedom of trade was followed closely by free movement of capital and this allowed multinational companies to grow rapidly. It meant also the proliferation of a network of international agencies, including banks, which were no longer so dependent upon the country of origin. There is also the European Investment Bank, which provides development finance in many Third World countries as well as funds for regional development, industrial modernization and transitional Community projects.

The "social" was always marginal to the development. This is illustrated by the Social Charter itself — which is workerist rather than collectivist in orientation. But, to do justice to the original six members, certain social assumptions — like collective bargaining, worker consultation and fairly high levels of support for dependent sections of the population — were taken for granted; though it must be emphasized that this was not so much planned as already provided by the individual welfare states of continental Europe. This gave a basis for consensus in taking decisions on behalf of competitive aggrandisement. But it has not been enlarged by EC measures and constitutional provisions. Economies of scale and rising levels of industrial production were central to the development. Fordism reigned at the heart of Community programmes.

Controlling multinationals

There were three major stages in this entire European development. Obstacles to market operations on the part of large corporations and multinational companies were swept away. Second, forms of democratic accountability were, by comparison with the political institutions of individual member states, meagre. And, third, few commitments were made to social developments, services or costs. These three now represent massive problems not just for the European idea itself, but for each of the member countries. They pose the daunting challenge which instruments like the Social Charter are intended to meet.

Let me briefly illustrate the three. First, obstacles to market operations were swept away. To serve the objectives of fair competition the Rome Treaty sought the removal not just of national tariffs but of national subsidies and regulatory devices. This suits multinational companies in various ways. There is the problem of transferring some control of prices from the state to the multinational companies. This has far-reaching effects in reducing national independence and control of the national economy. It also means that pricing of components of production can be varied to maximize profit and minimize taxation and other forms of control.

There is the problem of creating greater inequality of employment between regions and of eroding existing employment rights. Since 1979 the British Government has consistently pursued a policy of deregulation. The former Chancellor of the Exchequer, Nigel Lawson, said that the object of policy was to "remove obstacles to the effective working of markets in general and of the labour market in particular". But "part-time employment at low rates of pay, self-employment and various forms of casual work have also increased at the expense of full-time regular employment". There had been a "widening of pay inequalities and a lowering of labour standards", the "removal of the legal floor of rights to wages and employment", and the "inducement, through the tax and social security system, of low wage employment".

There are numerous specific examples. Treatment of the unemployed is one. Thus, "on the question of testing availability for work, the British rules appear relatively harsh. Some examples of other countries' rules show that several other countries offer job-seekers more choice and better protection from employers who offer substandard wages". Some analysts see examples from Britain as influencing steps towards privatization, decentralization and "debureaucratization" in the rest of Europe, and a drift towards a dual society created by the single market, which will consist of the uneasily secure and the marginalized poor.

So, in Britain, the deregulation laws and programmes introduced by the Thatcher Government have been widely condemned. In large measure, however, they are implicit in the structure and mode of operation of the European Community. The Social Charter embodies intentions that some member countries see as overtaking and perhaps leading to the replacement of already well-established employment rights in single nation states. After all, expressions of hope which please the poorer members may signal loss of rights and benefits to other members.

In the 1970s, following the admission of Britain to the Community, the Government gradually abandoned its own regional employment subsidies, including the regional employment premium. Those subsidies have been substituted by much smaller EC subsidies, which are also more widely dispersed. They are far less effective. One consequence has been the higher rates of unemployment which have prevailed in some of the regions with already high rates of unemployment. In the Community, dismantling of forms of social protection is authorized on the basis of free competition within the single market, while at the same time there are huge difficulties in drafting and implementing laws to substitute European for national provisions. In short, there is evidence of the erosion of fair employment principles.

This applies to new workers as well as existing workers. Action is being taken to harmonize immigration control. Britain anticipated 1992 with the Nationality Act 1981 and the Immigration Act 1988, with the effect of nearly stopping entry to the UK from the Indian sub-continent. Visa requirements have been imposed on visitors from Ghana, Nigeria, India, Pakistan and Bangladesh. It is argued that the immigrants who played such a crucial role in Europe's post-war developments are no longer needed. In fact, member countries are continuing to rely heavily on such cheap and flexible labour, and appear to be preparing the way, more consciously, for the substitution of nationals from the so-called Latin rim of Europe, and also from the emergence of a low paid and casual labour force within the midst of the original core of members. So it is not just the emergence of a two-tier Europe in place of labour market dependence upon the Third World, but also social polarization in most of the member countries which is at issue. The speed of the restructuring of industry is remarkable. In the steel, tyre, trucking and ship-building industries the number of companies is likely to be halved after 1992.

This is why the Social Charter and its Action Programme deserve a very mixed reception. It is tentative, restrictive in scope and needs to be bolstered. Thus, while recognizing certain vulnerable groups and demanding equal treatment for men and women, the Charter contains no corresponding call to outlaw racial discrimination. The process of deregulation in the 1980s has weakened the status of some minority groups of workers and has erected barriers to visitors, immigrants and refugees from outside.

Democratization

After measures to introduce easier market operations, the second stage of European development can be said to have been marked by the establishment of relatively weak and contradictory forms of democratic accountability. This can be said to have indirectly enhanced the powers of the market. Forms of democracy long-developed by individual member states assumed lesser importance once EC institutions began to operate.

Democratic accountability is badly served by EC institutions. The European Commission is the executive of the European Community and has the right to propose policy and frame legislation. Currently, there are 17 members (one for each of the 12 member states plus an additional five nominated by the five most populous states). They are nominated by member states, but are not responsible either to them or to the elected European Parliament. The members of the European Parliament have only an advisory role in relation to legislation although they can, if they operate collectively, make difficulties for the Commission unless their advice is heeded. The Council of Ministers consist of relevant existing ministers from the different member countries, coming together to discuss and approve the Commission's proposals. There is a system of qualified voting: member states are allocated votes according to size. The piecemeal development of democratic structures is now believed by some observers to be a major obstacle to desirable European development.

Social policy

The third stage in this evolutionary process has been the meagre backing for social development. The social is even more problematic than the economic and the political. European social policies are already skimpy. The Social Fund is much more narrowly based than originally intended and is limited to measures to relocate and re-train the European unemployed only. Its budget is only about 4 billion ecus or about 6 per cent of the EC budget. Few observers expect the Social Charter to have much influence on differential earnings, and even less on the adequacy of social security benefits.

In 1989, the EC budget was 44.8 billion ecus. This is less than half the social security budget, and less than the National Health Service budget, of the UK. And social policy comprises only 7.2 per cent of that budget (with the European Fund for Regional Development covering some of the employment subsidies, accounting for a further 9.6 per cent). The Common Agricultural Policy budget accounts for 67 per cent of the total. The entire anti-poverty programme of the Community is less than the social services budget of the county of Avon, where I live.

There is every reason, therefore, to regard EC developments with strategic dismay. To begin addressing 21st century social problems three major transformations are required: constitutional reform to enable democracy to operate coherently; constitutional reform to confer human and social rights; and legislation on social development and organization, with a corresponding upwards surge in budgetary provision. None of these things have much hope of early fulfilment. Our problem is that as the European Community grows in power — it is mainly a negative power to dismantle the national welfare states without much guarantee of what is to be put in its place. This is rather like a modern form of the introduction of the laws of enclosure — placing restrictions on certain individual rights and benefits previously enjoyed or earned by the people. The creation of an international welfare state is going to be a very long haul indeed.

Social policy has to be conceived in relation to the idea of social development rather than services and agencies dealing with social casualties. The problem is both cross-national and national. It will require new political initiatives, and a complex apparatus of positive institutional devices. I mean that principles of social development need to be knit into a statement of objectives which is less workerist than the Social Charter and more conscious of community at local as well as European level. Whether or not this will be successful will depend on tireless promotion by trades unions, political parties, city councils across Europe, and pressure groups — like Refugee Forum (an association of refugee self-help groups) and the Migrants Rights Action network (an alliance of migrant organizations with links to similar groups in Europe, which lately came together to "promote rights rather than collude with the 'begging bowl' approach favoured by a number of the institutionalized refugee agencies").

A social development programme augmenting and supporting a revised Social Charter needs to be produced for Britain. Our five-and three-year public expenditure programmes are inferior in range and comprehension to some of the national five-year plans of India, Malaysia and Kenya. Social development has never attracted to a similar extent the Government's recognition of the importance of economic development. Thus, there was the long-established National Economic Development Council. Proposals have been made in the past for a Social Development Council, to monitor social changes, review the interactive effects of different national policies, and contribute to the formulation of national social strategy.

There should be an International Social Development Council with an International or European Department of Social Policy headed by a government minister — working in close concert with MEPs. There might be national watchdogs for multinational companies and other institutions, requirements to produce reports on the social conditions and rights of employees in different countries; maybe representation on boards of management. These concerns gain from the growing interest in environmental issues throughout the world, and growing recognition, too, of the value of preventive policies.

A common social policy must make provision for structural transfers to deficit areas. This is unlikely to get very far without some semblance of an agreed incomes policy. Although the conditions for achieving such agreement seem, in the early 1990s, to be remote, the argument has to be put strongly to encourage debate to create such conditions. The evolution of a "fair" wage structure is crucial to the welfare not just of unions and their members throughout Europe but of the entire populations of member states. And whether there can be any restraint on maximum wages in that structure is more likely to have favourable results for the low paid at the bottom of that hierarchy than the introduction of a statutory minimum wage. Some kind of agreement could also be applied "generally to the financing of social protection: the geographical solidarity of today's family welfare policy compensating the geographical solidarity of the financing of tomorrow's retirements". But that necessarily means making the Social Charter, and the political setting for the reconstitution of that Charter, far less "workerist" than it is. It also means making multinational companies far more democratically accountable than they are.

The internationalization of British social policy is the greatest priority. If it does not take place, our politicians will become largely helpless observers of the remorseless social polarization and mass impoverishment which the single European market portends.

CHAPTER 11

Strategies for Growth

I
Employment Creation
Francis Cripps & Terry Ward

The European Community is now entering its third decade of slow growth and increased unemployment. This is accompanied by worsening social conditions in formerly prosperous areas, and the steady erosion of standards of social justice that have their roots in Western Europe's social democratic tradition. As the credibility of programmes for economic growth and social justice diminishes, so political support for left parties has ebbed away in favour of right-wing movements that legitimise individualistic and anarchic solutions to social problems.

Further development of the European Community is an absolute necessity for the European left. Without stronger Community policies there is no possibility of implementing a coherent programme to re-establish more dynamic growth, and provide a viable context for sustained job creation and more cohesive social policies.

The Community now seems to have reached an historical impasse. Maastricht provides a basis for developing the Community in the required direction. But, so far, preoccupation with securing ratification has diverted attention away from how the Treaty proposals can be translated into a practical framework for policy-making to deliver the objectives of more balanced economic development emphasized in the document. Governments of member states, themselves in crisis, seek to maintain credibility with national electorates by insisting on their primary position as representatives of national interest in the determination of Community policy, implicitly rejecting wider representation of regional and common European interests. National electorates, in turn, are suspicious of a Community where policy is determined

Map 1

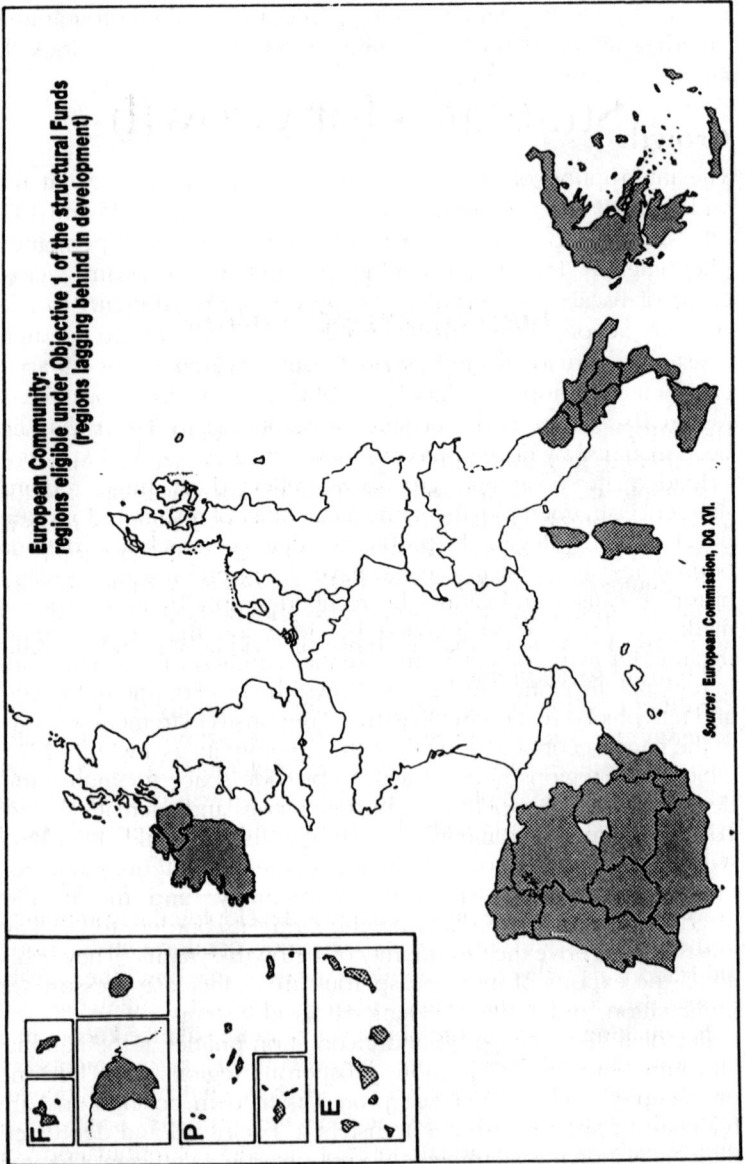

European Community: regions eligible under Objective 1 of the structural Funds (regions lagging behind in development)

Source: European Commission, DG XVI.

by horse-trading between governments of twelve independent member states. It is difficult for left parties to base their programmes on advocacy of a stronger Community when the Community lacks credibility with electorates.

Growth

The interruption of economic growth in the Community, at first widely seen as a temporary setback caused by the 1973 and 1979 oil "shocks", must now be recognized as a more permanent phenomenon. Two decades of low growth have locked in a vicious circle of fiscal crisis, eroding the power of governments to take positive action. They have caused long-term damage to areas assisted by structural funds. In "Objective 1" regions (see Map 1) economic development has been blocked, and in "Objective 2" regions (see Map 2) the closure of traditional industries has not been matched by development of new activities.

Inadequate economic growth is reflected in huge regional differences in unemployment and availability of resources for future development. Regional problems that cross both national boundaries and social classes have long-run and deep-seated historical causes and cannot be rectified simply by acceptance of market realities, as maintained by many on the right. A more dynamic growth context is an essential condition for a narrowing in regional disparities. As history shows, the level of unemployment and rate of job creation in Objective 2 regions is extremely sensitive to the rate of economic growth in the Community as a whole, while Objective 1 regions need growth to provide space for more rapid development of competitive export industries and to create jobs for young people and women who, in former times, would either have worked in agriculture or in the home. In the longer term, stagnation of problem regions within the Community, and the parallel stagnation of similar regions neighbouring its borders to the East and South, deprive the Community of a growth dynamic. They badly affect the exports of more prosperous areas, increase pressure for immigration, and undermine national fiscal systems.

Regional disparities profoundly condition politics at the national and European level. The more prosperous regions have become preoccupied with the need to protect their own position and are reluctant to pay for resource transfers to backward and depressed regions. National governments do not provide a sufficient channel for the representation of regional interests in the determination of Community policy. Although the preponderance of Objective 1 regions in Greece, Spain, Portugal and Ireland makes the national

Map 2

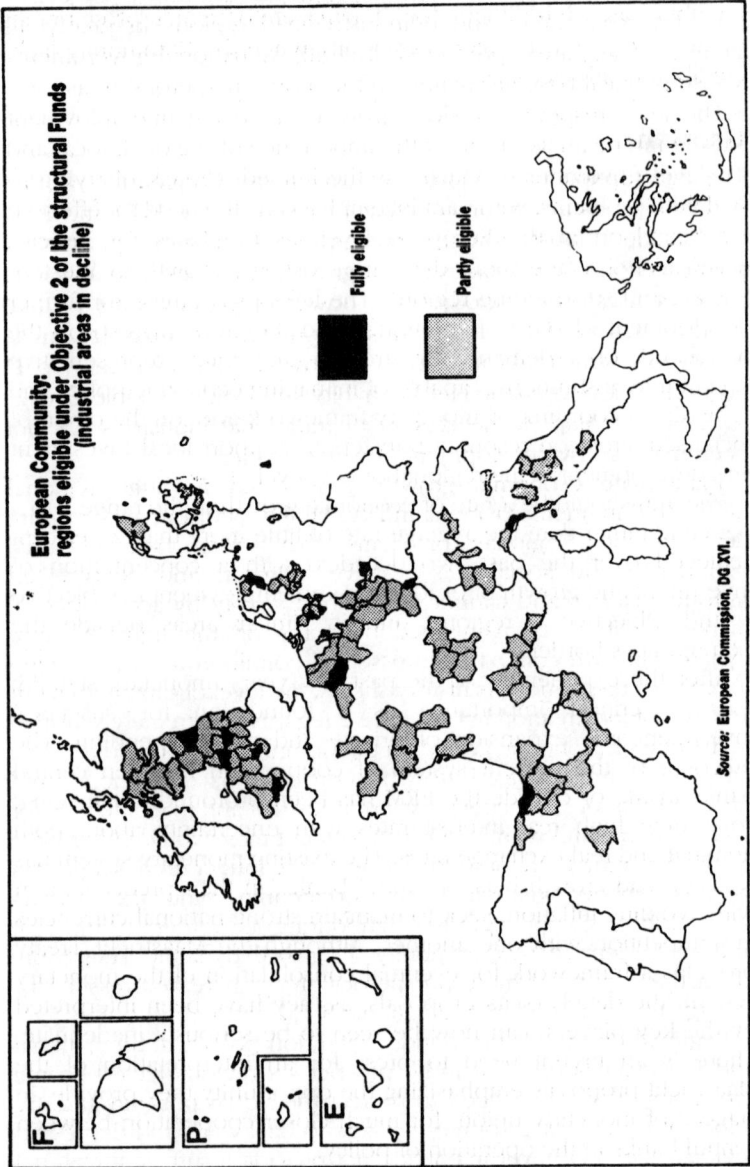

European Community: regions eligible under Objective 2 of the structural Funds (industrial areas in decline)

Fully eligible

Partly eligible

Source: European Commission, DG XVI.

governments of these countries into a significant lobby, Objective 1 regions elsewhere, and deindustrialized regions in nearly all member states, are represented, if at all, by national governments whose political base lies mainly in the more prosperous areas.

The left's response to slow growth and rising unemployment must combine an assertion of the importance of regional, local and city-level government, which has the immediate task of trying to deal with problems, with parallel emphasis on the need for effective representation at the European level, as the basis for policies necessary to secure more dynamic economic growth in Western Europe and surrounding regions. The left's programme for further development of the Community should therefore consist, on the one hand, of a demand for stronger and more representative Community institutions, capable of managing economic policy and providing a coordinated monetary framework and, on the other, of increased stress on resource transfers to support local investment and development at the regional or city level.

The aim should be a rate of economic growth in the range 3 to 4 per cent, rather than the average rate of little more than 2 per cent achieved over the past two decades, with a concentration of investment and growth of production and employment in Objective 1 and Objective 2 regions, and in similar areas outside the Community's borders.

After the experiences of the past few years, monetary stability assumes critical importance as a foundation for sustained investment and expansion of private and public spending. The outcome of the present system of cooperation between central banks inside or outside the ERM has been profoundly damaging, combining high real interest rates with uncertainty about both nominal and real exchange rates. The existing monetary system has a strong anti-growth bias as central banks, in their preoccupation with avoiding inflation, seek to maintain strong national currencies in competition with one another. Although the Maastricht Treaty provides a framework for eventual consolidation of the monetary system, the details of its proposals, as they have been interpreted by the key players, can now be seen to be seriously inadequate. There is an urgent need to press for an interpretation of the Maastricht proposals emphasizing the opportunity they provide, in Stage 2 of monetary union, for much closer cooperation between central banks in the operation of policy.

Common interests

It is essential that central banks should determine monetary policy on the basis of common European, rather than national, interests, and that monetary policy should be supportive, rather than restrictive, with respect to public and private deficits induced by recession. The function of the monetary system in a context of low growth and high unemployment should be to facilitate investment in infrastructure, improved social services and new business development; not to curb expenditure and bankrupt institutions already damaged by cuts in income. The anti-growth bias of monetary policy has been compounded by an anti-growth bias in attitudes to public spending. Public deficits have been universally regarded as harmful, despite the fact that in many cases they have been caused by downturns in private income and loss of confidence in private assets. Public debt has been forced up, to a large extent, by personal saving not being matched by sufficient business investment. In other words, so far from private investment being "crowded out" by government borrowing, public debt has been "crowded in" by a lack of confidence in private investment.

The bias against public debt, together with the weakness of national currencies within the EMS, has prevented governments from sustaining spending in recession, contributing to the long-term stagnation of economic growth, and depriving less prosperous regions of the cheap long-term sources of funds that would be required to start a new cycle of economic growth. If economic and monetary union is to provide the basis for faster economic growth it is essential that the union should have a sound system for public finance, encouraging stable long-term management of taxation and public spending, and protecting national, regional and local governments against deficits induced by recession. Long-term funding for public programmes needs to be accompanied by specific measures to recycle high private savings into sustained investment, especially in Objective 1 and Objective 2 regions. The redevelopment of these regions needs to be conceived in terms of partnership between city governments, local communities, local businesses and international companies, replacing the bureaucratic concept of partnership between Community, national and local officials on which existing structural programmes are based.

In parallel with structural investment, the Community needs a framework of legislation to promote job creation through encouragement of small businesses and employment-intensive services, such as those aimed at improving the environment or at meeting a range of social needs. Such discriminatory action, though at present contrary to the Single Market philosophy, need not damage the competitiveness of Community producers since it would be directed at businesses and activities not involved in international trade. Indeed, by encouraging the development of new ideas, it could strengthen competitiveness. If the large business sector continues to dominate the small, and if a substantial proportion of the population remains unemployed or inactive, the foundations for future prosperity are likely to be progressively eroded. Regions become heavily dependent on the ebb and flow of investment provided by international business and, therefore, remain at the mercy of developments over which they have little or no control. Unless small-scale, locally-based activities are legitimised and given some degree of financial privilege, it is impossible to see how contemporary demands for universal and flexible participation in the labour market can be accommodated.

In the longer term, the small business sector provides the fund of experience, new ideas and innovation that facilitates development of large businesses competing on a global scale. The key task now and in the future is to translate the need for policy action at the Community and local level into a concrete programme of action, defining not only the form and scale of measures that should be included, but, no less importantly, the parallel changes in political institutions and policy-making procedures that are essential if there is to be effective democratic control over decision-making.

Employment creation programmes

In parallel with structural investment in regions, where the pace of economic development has to be accelerated, there is a need to establish a framework of legislation to promote job creation through encouragement of small businesses and employment-intensive services. Even if GDP growth in the range 3-4 per cent can be achieved over the rest of the decade, this in itself is unlikely to create enough jobs to bring down unemployment to acceptable levels and, at the same time, provide work for the substantial numbers of women forced up to now to be inactive.

Moreover, outside of backward areas, where the need for economic growth and large-scale investment is acute, growth of production *per se* is in any event less of a priority. In many of the more prosperous parts of the Community, the challenge is to find alternative means of employment creation other than high growth rates. This means accepting the need to manage market forces so as to direct resources into activities that are consistent with the desires of people living in these areas for improvements in the quality of life and, at the same time, to ensure that this is not at the expense of job opportunities.

There is no shortage of activities that can potentially provide jobs while helping to achieve a range of social and environmental objectives. For example, the environmental industry in the Community, which in many areas is still in its infancy, is estimated already to employ over 500,000 people. It offers significant scope for expansion if finance was channelled into reducing pollution, waste management, water treatment, recycling and cleaning up both the natural and urban environment, and if the development of new production processes and new products in this area was encouraged.

Programmes to save energy and to develop new sources and to provide improved education, health, recreation and cultural facilities could together create considerably more jobs.

At the same time, there is a need to encourage the development and growth of small and medium-sized enterprises. This is not only important for the job opportunities that are directly created — often in a more satisfying working environment than large companies are able to provide — but, equally, for the longer-term competitiveness of the Community economy. In many sectors, small businesses provide the research and innovations to feed larger companies, which need continuously to improve their productive efficiency and introduce new products in order to be able to compete on world markets, but which lack the flexibility and individual motivation required to develop new ideas in many areas.

Moreover, because they are local in scale, small and medium-sized businesses are better able to respond to local labour market conditions and demands, including developing and exploring more flexible working arrangements — which might enable, for example, a given volume of work to be shared among increased numbers of people. In the Single Market, and in an increasingly unified financial market, however, small businesses will lose privileged access to local sources of funding, and are likely to find it more difficult to develop.

An effective employment creation programme, combining support for small business and the development of locally-based services, requires the establishment of a Community-level framework that leaves as much discretion as possible over the choice of local actions, but which, at the same time, defines the policy instruments that can be used, and the rules governing their implementation.

The fiscal system, in the form of indirect taxes, tax concessions, exemptions and allowances, as well as public expenditure on grants and subsidies, is the primary means of implementing structural policies in market economies. But given the mobility of business within the unified Community market, it is difficult for national, regional and local governments to use fiscal instruments for structural purposes in the absence of a framework defined at the Community level.

A good example is taxation designed to reduce environmental pollution and to increase the efficiency of use of limited natural resources. Although reduction of pollution and economizing on scare resources is of general benefit both to the country taking action and to others, if pollution or resource taxes are introduced unilaterally in any one member state, that member state faces the risk of losing business to others that are less careful.

Similar arguments apply to tax incentives that favour small and medium-scale enterprises, or taxes to fund improvements in education, health and social services, and so on. The increased tax burden on larger enterprises again carries the risk that business will be displaced to other parts of the Community where tax rates are lower.

Analogous arguments apply to the enforcement of minimum standards of health and safety and of working conditions as proposed in the Social Charter. Unless these are applied across the whole of the Community, businesses may tend to shift to areas where the authorities are most lax. Indeed, in the absence of an adequate mechanism for transferring income to problem regions to provide a significant incentive for business development, the responsible authorities may be tempted to use lax standards as a substitute means of attracting inward investment. The danger then is that, under pressure of competition, standards throughout the Community will gradually be reduced, and the hard-won advances in working and social conditions will be lost.

Key issues

The major issues arising from the above analysis that are central to a strategy for recovery and employment creation, and which, therefore, have to be the focus both of debate and political action, are as follows:

— how to establish sufficient democratic control and accountability of decision-making at the Community level to provide the basis for the coordination of economic policy that is essential for the effective pursuit of adequate rates of economic growth and employment creation in Europe, as well as for supporting development in neighbouring countries in Central and Eastern Europe, North Africa and the Middle East;

— how to rectify the defects in the ERM, demonstrated by the

events of the past few months, and establish an operational system with sufficient cooperation between central banks to provide financial stability with the flexibility required to allow for differences in economic conditions and performance between member states;
— how to establish a framework for the conduct of fiscal policy across the Community that ensures support for governments whose borrowing needs are increased as a result of downturns in economic activity, which avoids them being forced to cut public expenditure and/or raise taxes in recession and which, at the same time, helps them achieve longer-term budgetary goals without unacceptable reductions in spending that weaken their economic and social infrastructure;
— how to strengthen structural policy and ensure that there is a more direct and effective relationship between those responsible for managing both the structural funds and EIB investment at the Community level and the key players at the regional, city or local level, including private business — both large and small — as well as public authorities, who need to act in close partnership to provide an effective force for local economic development;
— how to establish a Community-level framework of fiscal instruments and other discriminatory measures to support small business and local employment creation and to exploit the potential job opportunities provided by the development of environmental and social activities, without damaging the international competitiveness of Community producers.

This section is extracted from a larger paper published by Spokesman as Europe Can Afford to Work. *The authors wish to thank other members of the Association for Applied Research in the European Community (ARCA), in particular, Ludo Cuyvers, Gerhard Leithäuser, Jacques Mazier, Pascal Petit and Enrico Wolleb, who provided valuable advice and material. None of these, however, bears any responsibility for the views expressed.*

II
Regional Recovery
Michael Barratt Brown

Nations and states

I am going to assume that we mean by regions the subdivisions of nation states rather than geographical groupings of nation states. There remains the problem of the definition of the nation state. Few states in the world are composed solely or even overwhelmingly of one nation, in the sense of a people sharing one language and a common history and culture. Most states comprise one or two peoples forming the majority with one or more minorities. The importance of this for our discussion is that regions in a nation state generally reflect national differences, as in the UK — England, Scotland, Wales and Ireland. Where there is one majority people and several minorities, it is also possible, if not probable, that the regions will be peripheral to the centre or in other ways enjoying a somewhat inferior status.

Developments in Europe over the last decade have involved the break up of a number of states — the Soviet Union, Yugoslavia and Czechoslovakia — into separate states based on the several nations contained previously within their borders. The rationale for this process of separation has been to give to the nation some greater measure of independence in managing its own affairs, especially in controlling its own defence forces and issuing its own money. Even where multi-nation states have not broken up, the claims of the separate nations for a greater degree of independence from the centre have been loud and clear. One can refer once again to the UK, but also note what has been happening in Spain, especially in relation to the Basque people and the Catalans.

It must therefore seem at first sight surprising that in the same period several of the nation states of Western Europe should be feeling their way forward towards some pooling of nation state powers in the European Community. This has created a major question in the minds of many people about sovereignty, supreme power, and what is called subsidiarity — that is to say the principle that matters which can be dealt with at a lower level should be dealt with there and only when they cannot be effectively dealt with there should they be transferred to a higher level. The principle has in fact been applied almost entirely to preserving the powers of the separate nation states from too much interference from the Community level, and very little has been said about giving power to regional levels below those of the nation state. Yet, as I have just suggested, the people may make special claims at these lower levels to exercise of political power on account of their separate nationality and special claims to economic consideration on account of their peripheral development.

In presenting the argument for a major place for regional development in economic recovery I shall be drawing not only on some British experience, but also on recent experience in Spain and a long connection with Yugoslavia going back to the war and immediate post-war years. I shall hope to show what may be learned from the two extremes of a highly centralised unitary state such as the United Kingdom and a largely decentralised federation such as Yugoslavia and from Spain which combines highly centralised elements with considerable decentralisation to the regions and provinces. I shall also be drawing upon studies I have been making on the problems created for African development by the inheritance from colonial rule of 56 nation states in one continent, 36 of them with populations of less than 10 million and 24 with less than 5 million. So that this is not just an academic exercise in political map drawing, I will try to indicate the main economic problems involved in distributing power between different levels of government in the European Community.

The historic division of powers between states and regions

Before we look at the arguments which have led economists to propose a major role for the regions in economic restructuring, we have to recall the historic origins of the division of powers between states and regions. In the development of European capitalism, the nation state emerged as a unifying and protecting force behind the challenge of a nascent bourgeoisie based upon the ownership of capital against the power of a feudal order based upon ownership of the land. Feudal rights and divisions had to be broken down so that land use could be altered, labour released from the land and the divisions between feudal land holdings destroyed so as to open up a single market to trade. To finance and defend the development of capitalist industry and commerce, local tolls and imposts and local currencies had to be ended and replaced by a central system of state taxation and borrowing and central control over the expenditure of a national money.

Where the aims of economic centralisation could not easily be achieved by a unitary state like the UK, federal states were created, as in the United States of America and the Federal Republic of Germany with some powers assigned by a constitution to the regions, but with the powers over external affairs and defence, the power to issue and control the money supply and the power to raise the greater part of the country's taxes reserved to the centre. This decentralisation of powers reflected the historic origins of local states or *lander* and their claim to recognition as in part self-governing entities. In a federation the degree of political decentralisation varies, most regions having their own legislatures and executive organs and some power to raise their own finances from taxation. This is what distinguishes them from a unitary state like the UK, where local government power to raise funds is strictly limited and can be withdrawn at any time, since it flows from central government authority. Spain, as I suggested earlier, reveals a half-way house, since the provinces and regions have their own parliaments and some constitutional access to funds, but only within a central state tax-system and central state budgets and central state control over local expenditure totals and even over major services like education and health. It has to be said that this centralisation of power in Madrid is very much resented and under challenge in Catalunia, the Basque country, Valencia and Galicia, which all have their own languages and traditions in many ways quite distinct from the majority Castilians. There is a similar movement of challenge in the UK to the centralised power of London from the regions of Wales, Scotland and Ireland, which again have their own languages and culture that are distinct from the dominant English. We can all think of similar situations in our own countries, where different nationalities are held within the boundaries of one state.

The arguments for a major role for the regions in economic recovery

The first argument for a major role for the historic regions in each state in the process of economic recovery is already clear. It is what the peoples of those historic regions will expect and, if recovery is carried out in ways that are insensitive to their expectations, they may turn to irridentist and disruptive activities. There are, however, powerful economic arguments for strong regional policies in any economic recovery. I have already suggested that many regions of multi-nation states which contain minority peoples are geographically peripheral and may be and generally are at lower levels of economic development than the majority people at the centre. This is not always the case; the Catalans complain about their lack of power because they are economically more advanced than the rest of Spain. The same was true of the Baltic republics in the old Soviet Union. The point of importance to be grasped is that the several regions in any single state are likely to be at different levels of economic development. In some cases, as in the Italian south, in the mezzo-giorno, in the Spanish west, in Extremadura, or in the south of Germany and southern Yugoslavia, an agrarian society at a lower level of economic development has a long history. In other cases, as in Scotland and Wales, Belgium and North East France, one-time strong industrial regions have become peripheral as the demand for coal and iron and steel and for the heavy industries based upon them has declined. Continuing decline of wealth and employment in such regions can lead to political tensions but it will also begin to undermine development in neighbouring regions.

A centrally planned command economy has the one merit that central government can shift resources from one region to another without difficulty. It has the great demerit that it is unlikely to do so when large vested interests have been established in existing centres of industry and existing industrial plants. Only in war-time are such interests likely to be challenged and in the early stages of industrialisation such problems of resource shifts do not arise. In a peace-time economy and after the first stage of industrialisation it becomes essential that old plant and unwanted industries are quickly dismantled and replaced by those that meet changed demands. Even if it were not wasteful of human energy and of natural resources, failure to adapt to new demands and to keep up with advances in productivity elsewhere soon leads to international uncompetitiveness, as became so abundantly clear in the Soviet Union and Eastern Europe. Unless nations are in a position to choose to follow a policy of autarky and to cut themselves off from international trade and commerce — an almost impossible route to follow in these days of ultra-fast communication, as the Chinese have discovered — national economies have to become capable of rapid adaptation if they are to survive.

By contrast with the planned economy, the unregulated capitalist market is an extremely efficient device for closing down unprofitable economic activities; it is much less efficient at ensuring that resources are quickly transferred to other uses and it is dangerously inefficient at encouraging new growth in declining regions. Such encouragement has always had to be provided by government intervention, which has frequently been inadequate and too long delayed. The result has been serious wastage of human skills and abandoned infrastructure of housing and services in one time prosperous regions while development has taken place in other regions which then needed new infrastructure to sustain them. Apart from the human dislocation and the wastage of resources, concentration and congestion of activity in favoured regions has aggravated problems of transport and environmental pollution. This weakness of the market system is part of its strength; it encourages development where there is the best land, the largest market, the greatest concentration of skills, the widest possibilities of external economies. This, of course, offers the best opportunities for growth — up to a point, but with the proviso that other regions which are left to die become increasingly poor markets for the new production of the favoured regions.

The tendency in market economies to uneven development has been worsening in recent years. Average incomes in different regions in the same countries, as well as between countries, have been polarising — the rich becoming richer and the poor becoming poorer (see Table 1). Such uneven development results in halting growth and it is likely to become cumulative unless remedial measures are applied. The danger of cumulative polarisation is much increased when markets which had been insulated from each other by local protection are opened up to competition. The single market in the European Community will lead to the elimination of all protective barriers, giving free range to the most advanced producers and the most favoured nations at the expense of the less advanced and less favoured. Short term growth can be expected to result, but with the long term consequences of failing markets for the products of the new growth. Nothing less than measures of income redistribution and especially of regional assistance will suffice to correct this tendency.

Nobel Laureate Professor Jan Tinbergen, writing in 1954, distinguished between negative and positive integration. Successful negative integration has been achieved in the breaking down of barriers to form a single market in the European Community to complete the common market, with a free trade area, customs union, free movement of capital and labour and a monetary union.

Table 1: European Community: Relative income per head, 1960, 1973, 1992

Country	Population (millions)	GDP per head at current prices and PPS (EC =100)		
		1960	1973	1992
Luxemburg	0.4	158.5	141.9	131.7
Germany	61 (+17 East)	117.9	111.1	113.6
Denmark	5	118.3	113.1	111.4
France	54	105.6	110.1	108.8
Belgium	10	95.4	101.2	103.4
Italy	57	86.5	103.0	103.2
Netherlands	13	118.6	113.1	102.7
UK	56	128.6	108.5	102.1
Spain	38	60.3	79.0	79.9
Ireland	3.4	60.8	58.9	68.9
Portugal	10	38.7	58.4	56.3
Greece	10	38.6	56.8	52.1
EC	336	100	100	100
USA	227	189.6	161.6	146.9
Japan	121	55.8	96.2	124.3

Note: PPS = Purchasing Power Parities
Source: European Commission, Annual Economic Report, 1991/2

Positive integration requires economic union with a single currency, common social policies and joint actions of regional development. In case this should seem to be a mere academic harking back to old-fashioned Keynesian redistribution theory, it may be appropriate to quote from two of the founding fathers of the European Community. The first quotation comes from the Spaak Report of 1956:

> "It is wrong to suggest that, when areas which have not attained the same stage of economic development are suddenly joined together, the lower cost of manpower and the higher return on investment automatically assure faster progress in the initially less developed region, leading ultimately to the alignment of economic levels. On the contrary, as shown by the Italian unification experiment after 1860 and in the United States after the war of Secession, the gap may widen cumulatively if the basic conditions are not met by public means.
>
> Positive and collective action, on the other hand, benefits the more developed areas too, for they share in the enhanced economic activity thus created, and it prevents the pressure on wages and standard of living which the connection with less developed regions might otherwise entail."

The second quotation comes from the Marjolin report of 1966, which maintained that:

> "the free working of the market is not in a position to assure a reduction of differences in regional prosperity, and the rsponsible authorities must initiate an active policy permitting the essential conditions for regional development and eliminating those distortions which favour regional disequilibrium. The creation of a unified economic area and the growth of trade with third countries intensifies competion between firms, with the result that various adaption problems, inevitable in any event, are posed more quickly than otherwise would have been the case in certain regions and sectors."

The importance of these two quotations lies not only in the strength of their argument and in the authority of their authors, but in the fact that they appear in the introduction to the most recent report on social cohesion and regional development prepared for the European Commission.

Structures of subsidiarity

Establishing the principles that wealth must be redistributed to prevent its accumulation into a few hands at the centre and that positive regional policies are needed to achieve this end is one thing. Ensuring that it happens is quite another. If it cannot be done by command, and the market will not do it, what economic structures are required for the purpose? Subsidiarity implies not just a placing under, but a placing above. This is obvious enough to nation state governments, where the threat to their power comes from below, from the regions; it is much less obvious when it comes from above, from federal or putative federal government. In either case, some structure is required to hold together the centre and the regions, the federation and the states, and it will not be acceptable for this to be by top-downwards commands.

Constitutions which assign precise powers to central and regional government, as in the USA or Germany or in Yugoslavia, have emerged out of specific historical circumstances. They cannot simply be reproduced in different circumstances. But one lesson seems to be clear. Powers were given to the centre for common action and not for joint action. That would be the nature of a confederation of equal state or regional powers; and it is hard to find a historically succesful confederation, whether we look at ancient Greece, the early United States, central Africa, the League of Nations or the British Commonwealth; and the Commonwealth of Independent States which has replaced the Soviet Union looks in no better case. The reason is not far to seek. Each state or independent region aims to preserve its own powers and special position. As the historian AJP Taylor put it to Bertrand Russell in dismissing his enthusiasm for the League of Nations, there appears to be no good reason why national leaders who work against each other outside the sessions of the League should suddenly discover that they want to work together when they meet in Geneva. The United Nations was designed to overcome this weakness by the creation of an international organisation with some powers derived from an abrogation of power by the member states. Joint action is not the same as common action. Attempts to arrive at joint action, as for example in the meetings of the G7 — the seven most powerful capitalist states in the world — have singularly failed to achieve anything. They have had no organisation to which to delegate power to act in common.

The lesson to be drawn from this experience for economic recovery in Europe seems to be that effective regional development, especially of backward regions, requires not only funding from the centre but a strong central organisation that is specifically concerned with regional development. This organisation will probably be a federal department with a secretariat or a para-statal body. It will have to be responsive to the particular needs of each region, and the actual use of resources must be in the hands of the regional authorities, but it cannot be a joint body representative of the several regions, or it will become a cock-pit of conflicting claims.

Paradoxically perhaps, decentralisation is only effective where there is strong central allocation of resources. This must, however, be carried out according to carefully constructed and agreed criteria, so as to avoid what the Americans call "log rolling" (you roll my log and I'll roll yours) and other conniving or corrupt practices.

Much can be learned for restructuring government on principles of subsidiarity from the practices of large modern companies. They have increasingly decentralised their decision making to "profit centres" at the lowest effective level, and between these centres they have encouraged net-working in place of coordination from above. By net-working is understood horizontal communication and the establishment of linkages that are not prescribed from above. Linkages are created and maintained by networkers, who are not directly responsible to higher authority, but work out from units at lower levels in a company structure. The network provides not only a system of communication but a regular system of connections inside the market between suppliers, often sub-contractors and major units in the company structure. Applied to local and regional government, networks provide essential links between consumers and producers of both goods and services. They allow for flexibility and local or regional variation of provision within a national framework of resource allocation. Through computer recording of transactions, central authority can be informed of what it needs to know about what is happening at the base, without having to give commands or interfere unless disproportions arise. Of course, the independence of the profit centres does not exclude the channeling of profits to the centre for overall decisions on investment. The same would be needed in a federal structure of government. (Some indication of the way networks can be used to complement and strengthen the working of the market while avoiding overmuch top downwards planning can be found in M. Barratt Brown, *European Union: Fortress or Democracy*, Spokesman for European Labour Forum, 1991)

The lessons from Yugoslavia

The awful experience of Yugoslavia offers extremely valuable lessons for those states which comprise several nationalities at different stages of economic development. After Tito's break with Stalin in 1952 central planning was abandoned and the economy was opened up to market forces. Most of the power over economic affairs was transferred to the republics and to self-managed enterprises owned by local authorities at different levels throughout the country, but still within the Communists' monopoly of political power. Local powers were still held firmly within a legal framework of taxes and norms set by the federal government. Economic development was subject to non-compulsory indicative planning, which the continuing monopoly of political power in the Communist League helped to assure. A crucial element in this framework was the regional development policy which had been regarded from the start of the new Yugoslavia as a key element in over-coming the nationalities question.

During the central planning period, resources were allocated to the regions for investment and for social and public services from the federal budget. Thereafter, the constitution continued to require that social services in the less developed regions receive a federal subsidy, but funds for development were allocated by a system of competition at first through a general investment fund, then through the banking system and finally through a Federal Fund for Crediting Economic Development of Less Developed Republics and Regions. The system always involved much log rolling by members of Parliament pressing the claims of their own locality and resulted in absurd duplication of plants, most of them running at well below full capacity. The Federal Fund was managed by an independent board of eight members, one from each republic and autonomous province, and it drew its funds from an obligatory contribution imposed upon all enterprises as a proportion of their social product. There is no doubt that up until the early 1970s investment was increased very rapidly in the two provinces of the Voyvodia and Kosovo, but outside these two areas Slovenia and Croatia achieved much more rapid growth of investment than the southern republics.

In 1974 a new constitution was adopted in Yugoslavia which decentralised power even further, not only to the republics and the provinces, but to the thousands of self-managed enterprises and "interest communities". The federal government had no influence over the expenditure and revenues of these. The Communist League provided the sole coordinating force. Most of the enterprises could make their own investment decisions and earn and spend foreign currency. Decisions relating to the Federation such as fiscal and monetary policy, taxation and public expenditure, social services and the contribution to the Federal Fund for Development were made by negotiation leading to agreement between the eight republics and provinces. The contribution was greatly reduced to a figure of no more than 2 per cent of the social product of enterprises and the social service subsidy to less than 1 per cent of Yugoslavia's national income. The gap between the richer northern republics and the southern poorer republics and provinces widened.

Meanwhile, the decentralization of power inside Yugoslavia meant that the federal government had no power to manage the movement of exports and imports or to control uses of foreign currency. The separate republics were increasingly unable to agree on common measures. To meet the foreign debt and to pay for its own spheres of operation and especially for defence, the federal government steadily printed more money. The rate of inflation rose from an average of 15 per cent in the 1970s to 40 per cent in 1981-3, to an average 200 per cent in 1985-8 and finally to over 1300 per cent in 1989. When the armed forces decided to back a strong man as leader of the Serbian communists to bring the situation under control, the Communist League broke up in bitter recriminations and the two northern republics broke away from the federation. The result has been civil war and an internecine struggle between Serbia and Croatia over the body of Bosnia and Hercegovina with its large Moslem population spread out among the Serbs and Croats.

The lesson for us of this tragedy is not, I think, that each nation should have its own state and its own money and its own armed forces, let alone clear other nationalities out of its territories. That makes no sense in a world of giant transnational companies and of two or three groupings of state power — in Europe, in the American continent and in East Asia. The lesson is rather that states which contain separate ethnic groups and have problems of regional disparities have to engage in strong regional development policies which are decided upon by central or federal government in the interests of the whole people, even though they are advised by regional authorities about particular needs and the policies are executed by these authorities or in many cases by lower local bodies on the true principle of subsidiarity. At the same time, the other lesson is that much wider federal arrangements are required at the European level, which will also make possible strong regional policies in the interests of the whole of Europe. These too will need strong central organs capable of ensuring that resources are redistributed from the richer and more developed to the poorer and less developed.

Finally, the principle of subsidiarity has to be extended still further upwards — to the very top. For the whole world to develop without growing disparities of income and wealth, an arm of the United Nations is needed, which is not dominated by any single power or group of powers, particularly not the richest, but acts in the interests of all the people of the world to ensure that wealth and income are more equally distributed. That must seem an utopian dream, so long as there are short term benefits for the rich in leaving things as they, whatever the disaster for their children. At least at the lower levels of state and nation where we are working, we can do something to create the consciousness of what can be done to strengthen solidarity and weaken the forces that are leading to division and disintegration.

References

Stuart Holland, ed. *Out of Crisis*, Spokesman, 1983.
The Regional Problem, Macmillan, 1976.
Capital versus the Regions, Macmillan, 1976.
UN Economic Commission for Europe, *Economic Survey of Europe, 1989-90*, Geneva 1991.
Economic Survey of Europe, 1990-92, Geneva 1992.
J-M Tortosa, "Personas al Margen", en VV.AA., *Los Espanoles del 92*, ed. A. de Miguel, Madrid, Alianza, 1992.
Iraj Hashi, "The Disintegration of Yugoslavia: Regional Disparities and the Nationalities Question", *Capital and Class*, no.48, London, Autumn 1992.
M. Barratt Brown, "The War in Yugoslavia and the Burden of Debt", in Ken Coates (ed.) *Drawing the Peace Dividend*, Spokesman 1992.
"Defending the £ or Expanding the Economy", in *European Labour Forum*, Winter 1992-1993.
Short Changed: Africa in World Trade, Pluto Press for the Transnational Institute, London, 1992.
Ken Coates, "European Recovery Programme", in *European Labour Forum*, Winter, 1992-93.
Zhivko Pregel, "Economic Reform" in *Review of International Affairs*, no.956, Belgrade, February 1990.

III
Reforming Working Lifetimes
Regan Scott

European unemployment poses a momentous challenge to trade unions. This is because the scale of the job creation problem goes well beyond previous drives for shorter working hours, beyond the best traditions of campaigns around the 35 hour week objective that characterized the 1980s.

The issues were clear then. There was a persistent optimism about the right to increased leisure in a wealthy, if problematic, world. There was the imperative of solidarity, expressed in the belief that shorter working hours would create extra work. There was a simple, popular demand: reduced weekly hours plus some annual holiday targets. Bargainers faced up to the problems of trade-offs between higher pay and shorter hours, but the basic perception remained one of eventual increases in real incomes. There was a clear public argument about job creation, and time to adjust to what looked like a natural process, if only it could be pushed along. Unemployment looked still to be composed of cyclical factors, run downs in old industries, imbalances in job creation and other structural factors amenable to sensible labour market interventions, no more radical than had been practised by the Swedes for many years. Even the anti-inflationary factor in unemployment, driven by monetarist doctrines, looked to be capable of reversal, especially since some countries with monetarist regimes seemed to be able to hold employment levels fairly high.

It is the disappearance of this scenario that poses the momentous challenge to European unions. The formal commitments, the basic morality, the bargaining skills remain in place, but power has shifted in the market place for work, and politics has moved on into a more threatening and diverse pattern. Underlying these shifts, driving them, has been the arrival of fully fledged global competition, marked by the discovery of advanced capitalist cost-saving mechanisms in employment far outstripping the job replacement forces of new capital and government-led investments and expenditures. If we were in an era of needing Keynes Plus in the 80s, the "plus" now needs to be very big indeed. Above all, its need big scale worksharing to see anything like full employment on the horizon again.

The analysis offered by the European Economic Recovery Programme team has put up the essential long-term arithmetic. It has unveiled a special feature of the coming era, namely, the threat of growing unemployment on top of existing levels if economic growth simply recovers a low/modest technical recovery path. The explanation can be put simply: economic recovery from the current deep cyclical depression will be competition-led, and impede its own potential by displacing more labour. That is, unless action can be taken to boost demand to a high growth path, and shorter working hours can redistribute some of the work and hence income flows.

A new era of unemployment?

The sense of a new era of unemployment haunted the speech made by Jacques Delors at the European Parliamentary Socialist Group's Conference in February in Brussels. Delors asserted the need for a "new development model" with which to respond to the unemployment challenge. He proposed a new drive for shorter working time, talked of a new "consciousness of leisure and work sharing", of the massive job potential in environmental areas. He asserted that union leaders had been "courageous" (over the relationship between pay, productivity and competitiveness) in the 1980s, but in the new circumstances he questioned whether anyone was now clear what real trade-offs are being offered to employed workers. Unions had become socially conscious, but needed to develop new trade-off demands. It is a perspective reflected in the work of the European Metalworkers Federation's Collective Bargaining 2000 Programme, although the gravity — immovability — of the unemployment problem has still to be digested by unions representing the stronger economies of the 1980s.

A strong tradition

Looking back at the great tradition of shorter-working-hours demands in the trade union and socialist movement might prove more than a formal archival exercise; looking forwards to the demand for a 1000 hour working year might prove more than a utopian impulse. Certainly there is a large gap between the current target of a 35 hour week, and the millennial 1000 hour year. It's a very big gap compared to the move from the ten-hour-day demand to the eight hour demand. But perhaps our thinking needs to be more flexible, more responsive to social choice and innovative patterns of hours management. What, for example, has happened to the demand for a four day week, which I recall being insisted on alongside the 35 hour demand by my own union when the modern drive for shorter working time was launched in the very early 1970s?

The history of concrete action provides a positive backdrop. The German Metalworkers Union's campaign for the 35 hour week in the mid 1980s was pursued rationally, with an impressive build up and preparation of the case, and was prosecuted with a ruthless industrial logic through selective strike action. The subsequent engineering industry campaign in the United Kingdom for a 37 hour week, a reduction of the longstanding 39 hour week, also used selective strike action, resting on a hugely successful special strike levy fund — it collected £19 million — and finishing up with a surplus of £7 million now available for another campaign. Strike pay was set at £100 a week — a revolution in organized support levels for UK manual workers. 1,300 agreements were negotiated for a two hour reduction with "no strings" and 600,000 workers were covered. The campaign started in September 1989 and the levy was suspended in December 1990 on the basis that "stage one of the 35 hour week campaign . . . proved so successful . . ."

From the viewpoint of public awareness and political debate, the coincidence of the European Economic Recovery debate with the expected implementation phase of the modest but procedurally progressive European Working Time Directive provides an ideal space for the development of new demands and perspectives.

Essential features

Action requires more than arithmetical forecasting, more than new economic rhetoric, and more than the sustenance of past progress. At the very least it requires a close scrutiny of existing analyses and their related action programmes to see where concrete new approaches are needed to meet a challenge on a new and much bigger scale.

First, the trade-off of pay against shorter hours during the 1980s will need to be re-examined. Employers seem to have absorbed the extra costs that they persistently argued would make their products uncompetitive, making productivity gains from the work reorganizations that followed shorter hours. Equally, the question of assessing the job creation side of shorter hours needs to be looked at very carefully. While no one expects a fully proportionate gain from shorter hours, where unit cost advances are being made from reorganization, the possibility of market expansion creating new jobs needs to be added into any assessment.

Certainly, bargainers who moderated their pay demands to make progress on shorter hours are unlikely to accept the old analysis again. Real wage increases therefore need to run in parallel with advances in shorter hours, not behind them.

Second, given that union bargaining power will continue to be seriously limited by persistent unemployment, the likelihood of advances in shorter working hours by key sections pushing ahead and weaker ones following on needs to be examined. At worst, some sections of advanced industry and services might make progress, only to find that the overall effect at macro level is an increasing gap in normal working hours between core and periphery workers, between strongly organized and unorganized sectors. Unions will therefore need to step up their social campaigning to maintain solidarity across the different sections of the organized workforce.

The social dimension of reducing working time therefore needs to have an even more prominent role as a complement to limited progress on sectional issues. The increasingly recognized and massive constituency of women workers — most new jobs are for women, and most of them are poor jobs, often in "atypical" categories — should mean that women's demands on hours can move from being sectional to be being mainstream, and potentially hegemonic, depending on the degree of union organization amongst women. Other examples of socially specific parts of the workforce could provide similar potential.

Third, the pace of changes in productivity can be very rapid. Coal miners in Britain, for example, doubled their productivity in eight years. High increases in productivity from corporate and sectoral restructuring leave workers experiencing efficiency as redundancy. This is not a successful growth path. It can also mean that some corporations boost profitability without need of expanding markets, that is, efficiency without growth.

Fourth, union co-operation with the flexibility demands of advanced production techniques will need to be re-examined, with more stress placed on countervailing demands for security. This is both a matter of trade union bargaining practice, and also a matter of macro labour market analysis, as mentioned above. A new concept of "flexible security" will need to be developed for both bargaining and labour market policies. The heavy economic costs of excessive external labour market flexibility need to be assessed. In periods of heavy and prolonged unemployment, job exits and entries have been affecting approximately three times the numbers of people recorded in unemployment figures. A recent *Financial Times* survey suggests that 1 in 4 workers in the UK experienced at least one bout of unemployment in the two-year period from 1990 to 1992, while the stock of unemployment was around 10 per cent. Rights to job security for the massive peripheral workforces of economically advanced countries will need to be put centre stage. There is a good basis here, in representing the massive underclass of atypical workers, for developing the European Community's "fundamental rights" concept to unify different categories of worker. My own union's pioneering campaign for permanent rights for temporary workers and full time rights for part time workers needs to be pressed strongly on to the European agenda at programme level.

There is a further aspect to employment that is both "time flexible" and "time limited" — atypical employment. This needs to be perceived as exploitative not simply in terms of low wages and overhead social costs, but also in terms of the time dimension. The relative time security of regularly employed workers, with attendant redundancy costs that can be quite high, has become a serious threat to restructuring capital. In the current imbroglio in the United Kingdom about "transfers of undertakings", the capital costs of redundancy play a central part. Public sector employers and private sector subcontractors are trying to off-load redundancy costs on to each other in an impossible project of social cost avoidance. The same point applies also to pension costs, although recent European Court decisions have been helpful in the setting of "transfers of undertakings".

Fifth, redundancy payments nevertheless need to be reviewed in the light of the relative ease with which workforces have been restructured. The calculator base for redundancy has been historic, built on by collective bargaining pressure. A more socially responsible accountancy is required to make job reductions punitively expensive.

Bringing redundancy costs into the same ball park as job creation costs (they are very high for productive/traded/competitive jobs) would be a useful strategic exercise. The outcome of such an approach might be enhanced lay-off rights and rights to return to jobs. These could prove especially attractive as well as being socially progressive since increasing numbers of workers in flexibilized labour markets will not have much in the way of service with any single employer to put into their redundancy calculations. It is worth noting here that the fascination of the 1970s with regard to redundancy compensation as a "worker's property right in their job" would become a wasting asset as a sanction in the current era of persistent mass unemployment and volatile labour markets.

Sixth, the powerful reality of global competition by excessive working hours needs to be taken on board in policy and political demands. The economists' customary equation of wages and output making up unit costs as the competitive index of efficiency /productivity differences needs the injection of a third, classical ingredient: working hours. This would give us a proper index of undercutting and unfair competition from high working hours economies. The global figures are:

Japan: 2,050 annual hours, in reality, nearer 2,400 hours

USA: 1,800 hours

European Community: 1,700 hours average

Germany 1,550 hours

(see *Financial Times* 11/12 May 1992)

(A 35 hour week and five weeks' holiday plus public holidays produces a working year of approximately 1400 hours).

Japanese hours are long and include unpaid overtime, often unrecorded. USA hours, especially for salaried workers and the self employed, have risen since the 1960s. The trend pattern of hours in the global economy is no longer one of the relative speed of reductions in advanced economies. Observers of some Japanese transplant companies suggest that they will be sorely stretched to meet the European Community's eventual 48 hour week requirements.

Seventh, global competitiveness needs to be examined for further characteristics: the retention of routine and substantial margins of excess capacity as a competitive weapon and the development of routinely available customized reserve armies — or brigades — of workers. It is an important perception to understand.

Eighth, such is the complexity of working patterns, the spread of actual hours worked across Europe, and the trend to flexibility of time within whatever agreed patterns exist, that attention needs to be given to the formulation of basic demands.

One obvious but relatively new proposition is that this could take the form of an annual hours target. The European Economic Recovery Programme makes its calculations as economic arithmetic, not as a set of demands. The necessary scenario for moving back to effective full employment in Europe involves an across-the-board reduction of two hours in working time throughout Europe.

Debating a menu of shorter-working-time demands

Given the wide disparity of basic and worked hours across Europe, a two hours' salami slice off all workers' hours would be a neat solution. But life is not that simple. The realities of adaptive processes suggest that a socially attractive and unifying demand is needed.

This was certainly the case with the 35 hour week demand, which took hold in the advanced metal and engineering industries, as pathbreakers for other sectors. What the German and British campaigns showed was that a two hour reduction in working time can be accommodated without dislocation and crisis.

The European Economic Recovery Programme forecasts do not require excessively dramatic action. The necessary work-sharing arithmetic could be achieved on a phased basis over time, and it is fair to argue that, if the economic case is put strongly enough, and political support can be mobilized, then the reversal of a secular trend against reduced working hours at the global level would be a major achievement in its own right.

The key demand must be the creation of a more level playing field in hours of work, and, in principle, the common sharing of reduced hours. The demand for work sharing against unemployment is, by definition, egalitarian. There would be little point in the new integrated single European market place for labour having a high productivity/short hours sector in a few countries counterbalanced by long hours in the newer member states. Capital would simply switch its investment location. The case of the transfer of Hoover jobs from France to Scotland points up the role of working time in competition. In this example, it concerned the transfer of full time jobs into time-limited contract ones: two years and finished, exploiting the United Kingdom's pernicious two year waiting time for legal job protection.

However, a common salami-sliced reduction may not be attractive in all countries, and may not be amenable to implementation where working time management through collective bargaining is weak. I can see no special solutions here, more the need for a debate about methods of implementation, working back from a global target at the end of the century of, say, 1200 annual hours, including a common paid training time allowance.

The option of a linked 35 hour/four day week formula, referred to above, has some obvious merits. When it was formulated, it had the tactical attraction of relating to existing patterns in the car industry in the United Kingdom of working a short fifth day at the end of the week. There was also a lay-off resonance, and an associated idea that leisure time might be maximized if taken in blocks rather than on a daily basis of leaving work 20 minutes earlier, only to find oneself in the same traffic jams. This would establish the principle of maximizing the social usefulness of reduced work time.

The obvious fear is that an annualized unit of working time might lengthen the working day and working week. This is why no single demand can stand up front. Protection is needed for the rest period within the working day, between working days, and within the working week. This trend of thinking is already in evidence in the European Community's Working Time Directive[1], which is, significantly, awaiting the resolution of an argument about the rival merits of a three and a six month reference period for averaging out the 48 hour legal ceiling. While there are grave concerns about the particular periods specified in the Directive, it nevertheless provides a precedent for posing multiple demands that give considerable scope for practical application subject to collective bargaining, a key principle being pressed by the European Trade Union Congress on behalf of its affiliates. This takes the specific form of a demand that any derogations from the Directive should only be allowed if agreed by the unions through collective bargaining.

On the other hand, the case for the annualization of hours becomes more relevant the greater becomes the reduction in basic hours and the more complex the patterns of cover become for production requirements. The notion of the standard day has been culturally eroded by the extension of shift working into 24 hour cover and 7 day cover in many industries. That trend took place in the 1970s and 1980s, and while it may have come about without as much gain in shift and disturbance payments as might have been won, nevertheless it is now an irreducible fact.

This is a social fact as crucial as the needs of women and men as parents for flexible working time, and similar cases such as the needs of people on training courses, of carers, and of many other time-tied sections of the workforce. These social dimensions might be easier to specify in annualized terms.

Finally, of course, annual holidays are naturally specified across the 52 weeks of the year, although considerable tension exists in many industries about the precise application of the holiday periods. There is a fair spread in annual holiday entitlements across Europe; a harmonization programme is an obvious part of the menu of shorter-working-time demands.

Towards an Action Programme

The essential ingredients of a working strategy are not difficult to delineate:

First, at advanced collective bargaining level, in the metal/ engineering industries, for example, the key issue will be to establish a working hours reduction and harmonization programme in European companies. The Maastricht provisions for European Works Councils and for "framework agreements" are natural instruments that have the attractions of involving both legal enforcement and collective bargaining.

Second, the European Economic Recovery Programme forecast assumption of a two hour reduction of working time across the board for all European workers needs to be transposed into a practical arithmetic. This might be expressed, for technical and social mobilization reasons, as an annual hours target figure for key dates like the Maastricht Treaty review date of 1996, the Year 2000, and/or the European Economic Recovery Programme's Community Budget Projection dates of 1997 and 2002. This is highly professional work, which could well be resourced by the European Community and conducted through "social partner" mechanisms. However, relevant protections for the customary units of working time need to be formulated, building on the EC Directive pattern, so that progressive goals are also set for the working day, the working week, annual holidays, and social leave.

Third, the arithmetic of necessary training time needs to be assembled for a high growth, full employment Europe. A number of training rights formulae exist, ranging from the starting demand specified by the TGWU/GMB unions in Britain for 5 days training time per year per worker. This reflects the existing low UK average, but would be revolutionary for most unskilled production and service sector workers. Other approaches can be generated on the basis of equal rights to quantities of training and social funding, drawing on the time spans needed for multiskilled craft workers and higher education students. An annualized arithmetic is needed by the European Economic Recovery Programme for macro-economic forecasting; a personalized arithmetic is needed for basic worker rights; a social cost arithmetic is needed for figuring out the required investment and demand creating dimensions of a coherent European industrial training strategy.

Fourthly, there is a clear need for a new treaty base to the European Community's working hours concerns. The Working Time Directive is based on health and safety principles. The case needs to be developed for broadening working time rights to include social needs, to enable unfair competition complaints on the basis of excessive hours (a "social clause" approach), and to establish paid time for training rights on a substantial level. Sabbatical leave rights, unpaid personal leave rights (to return to a job, as with maternity rights at present) — a whole host of demands need to be formulated and marketed to erode normal working time levels.

Fifth, the "social dialogue", Europe's own industrial relations lubricant, needs to be turned to the consideration of representations from a whole gamut of people and representative organizations in and around the labour market. Women, parents, pensioners, early retirers, youth organizations, trainers and their student customers — all need to be brought into the debate about working time and work related time.

The responsibility for work sharing on the scale required by a return to full employment cannot be off-loaded, or "subsidiaried", to regularly employed, unionized manual workforces in large enterprises. Their leading role canot be a sole role. The Herculean task needs to be placed on as many shoulders as possible to build up a vast menu of demands and possibilities — a new social settlement about socially productive time.

Beyond the Social Chapter

The direction is clear. Optimistic demands have to be made, but, at the same time, the back door has to be kept firmly shut. Rather than rejecting and vilifying the coming Working Time Directive, strategy should concentrate on a new conceptual basis for advances on a twin track with the new 48 hour ceiling providing the long stop.

The underlying argument here is clear: the Social Charter and the Social Chapter and earlier labour market Treaty Articles are now out of time. The era of permanent mass unemployment is with us. If more prosperous times provided a powerful argument for a Social Charter and a Social Chapter, workers in Europe now need a Social Revolution and a whole new social encyclopaedia.

Footnote

1 The measures contained in the European Community's Working Time Directive include a 48 hour maximum week spread over a reference period of 3 to 6 months (still to be decided), with a right to refuse overtime above this. Eleven hours minimum daily rest periods, average night work limit of 8 hours, 4 weeks minimum annual holiday, official notification of regular nightwork, and, for the UK, a register of workers volunteering to do overtime above 48 hours.

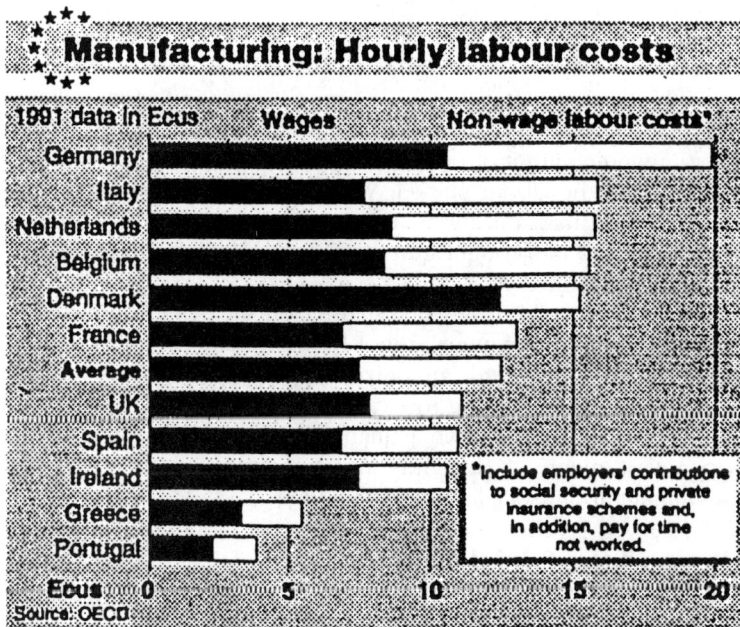

Source: *Edward Balls article in the* Financial Times.

IV
Linking Working Time with Recovery
John Hughes

There is a double sense in which a strategy for working time in Europe is needed. It is important to recognize that there are direct links with European recovery that cannot be neglected. Not least, these should connect with policies of other kinds to reduce the massive overhang of structural unemployment that disfigures our societies and denies rights; just as the unemployed are shut out from the rights and opportunities of the world of work. But there is another sense in which a strategy for working time can help to recover some degree of confidence in the European Community itself and its social policies. Inertia and bemusement in the face of openly reactionary labour "policies" of the UK Government is not a credible posture for a Commission — and those countries — that saw the Social Charter as expressing the "social identity" of the Community. It will not be possible to recover any adequate momentum for the coherent development of European institutions unless a renewed and more vigorous social programme is brought into being. And that can hardly prosper without measures that cumulatively reach out to offer a prospect of new balances between working life, and a wider creativity in social living.

It could be argued that putting together a programme linked to working time is, at this juncture, both utopian and subjective. Yet there is a sense of objective reality about each of the elements of a programme sketched in what follows. None of the issues raised can be denied a place on the agenda. Taken together, they open up a coherent development that could attract not only material resources, but the commitment of working people and their organizations.

Working Time Directive

It makes sense to start with the Working Time Directive. This should be put through with a sharper focus, and without emasculation. It should be recognized that this will involve majority voting, and that it must be defended as a measure that is most directly and properly concerned with health and safety. It should not be re-routed through the Maastricht protocol of the eleven (that is, excluding the UK), since one of its central tasks is actually to set limits to the de-stabilization of the UK labour market.

This means that a number of so-called compromises (actually capitulations), which were discussed by Social Affairs Ministers in

July 1992, should be abandoned. The European Parliament should play a major part in the arguments involved. The most flagrantly reactionary move was to accept the UK suggestion that individual workers should individually choose whether to work longer than 48 hours. Allegedly, workers who did not want to work more than 48 hours "would be guaranteed protection against pressures to force them to do so". (*The Employment Gazette*, July 1992). What hypocrisy! How do they become "workers" in the first place? Imagine a job interview. Candidate A is asked his/her views on working over 48 hours, and indicates unwillingness. Candidate B responds by "volunteering" to work longer hours. Who gets the job? More generally, the proposal is a blatant piece of sexual discrimination. As we have seen, relatively few women workers, compared with male employees, work excessive hours: and, doubtless, even fewer wish to do so. 48 hours already represents some eight to ten hours above the standard (basic) week that operates in most other countries of the Community. What is needed is a proposal to guarantee protection to workers, and this, in practice, would particularly mean women workers, who do not wish to work overtime beyond the standard week. Do we really want such workers to have no protection, by way of a European minimum standard, against "pressures to force them" to work more hours until they reach 48 hours?

It is also important to resist the "derogations" from the original force of the Directive that now disfigure it. It is particularly reprehensible to except inland transport from the Directive; if anything, the health and safety argument applies doubly here. There is the high risk of accident to workers, and other dangers to health, and also dangers to the travelling public. What is needed is provision for an agency, or national agencies, to permit derogations only within strictly negotiated and monitored limits, where a significant efficiency/service continuity case can be made — which cannot be met in other ways — and with strict requirement for "compensatory rest", and so on. The quid pro quo for even such a provision should be earlier conformity with the Directive than currently envisaged. The initial "derogation" in favour of collective agreements was a poisoned chalice for the trade union movement, as it should have recognized by now. All sorts of employers are now seeking to lumber through that breach of the Directive's principles and practice.

In addition, the Commission should press forward with a more extensive research programme, identifying health and safety issues — and stress is part of that — involved in new working time patterns. One important factor to recognize is that the combination of changing shift times, with pressure for overtime, (which may mean extra shift working) is particularly damaging, not only to health, but to family stability (not least when both partners are caught up in such patterns of work). Shift workers should be compensated by shorter annual working time, and in their case the 48 hour maximum seems excessive.

Part-time workers

The Commission must return urgently to its earlier — but substantially frustrated — programme to eliminate exploitation of part-time workers, and to challenge discrimination against them, whether by nation states (for example, through high thresholds of weekly hours in protective labour legislation or social benefits), or employers. Regrettably, this may only be possible in a strong form by utilizing the Maastricht social protocol to allow the members of the Community, other than the UK, to develop social measures with the full force of the Community law, but not operating in the UK. This would make much more visible and explicit any continuing discrimination on, for example, pension rights, training opportunities, and so on, by UK employers and the UK state. It would particularly put pressure on Euro-employers — those employing workers in more than one member state — if they practised double standards by discriminating against their UK part-time workers/temporary workers, and so on. It must be emphasized that discrimination against part-time workers is overwhelmingly a denial of equal treatment and equal opportunities to women workers, and the most important breach of the underlying principle of equal treatment for men and for women. As the Commission has succeeded in some parts of its programme on behalf of part-timers and temporary workers — notably in the health and safety framework Directive, and those Directives linked to it — it should monitor most vigorously to ensure that all member states are fully meeting the relevant commitments to such workers in actual industrial practice.

Young people

A concerted programme is needed at national level — but backed strongly by Community infrastructure funds — to delay young people's entry into the labour market in the most constructive way, by opening and widening access to relevant skill endowment, and deepening educational understanding.

It is already evident, comparing the rates of unemployment of young people in the current economic recession with that in the proportions "staying on" in full-time education and training. The numbers and proportions of the age group in further education and higher education are rising. But it is still a matter of what more can be done, given the numbers of young unemployed, and what can be done better, given the stretched resources and inadequate achievement of many of the educational institutions involved. Besides, in the more unregulated labour markets there is a risk — more than a risk — that employers will substitute "cheap" juvenile labour for more adult workers, so that overall employment does not rise, and overall labour income, and its purchasing power, may fall.

To illustrate the current situation, from Britain there were, at the beginning of 1993, 230,000 "claimant" unemployed young people aged 18-19 — this measure understates the real level of unemployment — and over 600,000 aged 20-24. It is still the case that fewer than half of 17 year olds are currently in full-time education or training. This is one of the lowest ratios in the European Community. The Government has provided funding for what it claims should be an increase of 250,000 in the student numbers in further education colleges over the next three years. However, the reality is that many such colleges are overcrowded and under-resourced. The fact that there are problems of quality is underlined by a recent Audit Commission report, which showed more than one in three further education students failing to finish their courses. In a similar way, the British higher education sector is expanding numbers, but lacks adequate resources to raise, or even maintain, standards, while grant support for students is being reduced — and has been over recent years.

Given the overall inadequacy of language teaching in Britain, and the importance of establishing a high level of understanding of information and communication technology and skills, there is much more to be tackled besides the traditional agenda of technical and occupational skills, and the wider pursuit of advanced science and the humanities. That is, therefore, a crucial element in the strengthening of the economic and social infrastructure of Europe. What else can be done?

The European Commission should be ready to do much more than hitherto to sustain and strengthen educational institutions whose thrust is to support and encourage the coherence, effectiveness, and imagination of European society and economic development. Regional and structural funds should be used to level up standards in economically disadvantaged areas; this should include both physical and human resources, linked to matching funds in the nations concerned. European lending institutions should be assisting, particularly where consortia of further and higher educational institutions in a region seek to pool and co-ordinate their physical and other resources — including student accommodation. The recent lop-sided boom, with its waves of property development, means that much recent large scale development is under-used or unused. Some of these could be adapted to meet the massive educational resource needs that an adequate programme of development would require. Member states facing acute problems of public sector financial management would be able to do more — and sooner — in strengthening the human resources of the Community, and the skill endowment of its labour force, if the European lending institutions moved substantially into relevant support for the educational infrastructure of Europe. In such a context, European understanding would benefit if one emphasis in such programmes was a dramatic increase in linkages between educational bodies in different Community countries, so that study for a period outside their country of origin became a normal feature of the education and training of the age cohorts that will be entering the European labour market in the later 1990s.

At the same time, the Community should move to check the thoughtless exploitation of young workers, and insist on linking working time with significant programmes of educational development as well as occupational training. In this context, a much greater emphasis could be placed by governments, by financial inducement, as well as example in the public sector of employment, on the large scale development of job sharing as a feature of the labour market for young workers. The real opportunities that exist are barely being developed at all. We have not even prototypes of the large scale, humane and imaginative programmes that need to be developed. The Commission itself should urgently encourage and disseminate "best practice" in this crucial area of young people entering the labour market, and give strong support to analysis and research, including major operational research programmes in co-operation with the social partners.

We have been urgently reminded by recent developments of the sacrifice and waste of the younger generation in Europe in war. The Community cannot shirk the task of avoiding waste and sacrifice of the younger generation through unemployment and economic and financial inertia.

Older people

Just as Europe needs to rethink its categories in planning the entry into the labour market of its young citizens, so it is failing to meet, with sufficient imagination, the needs of its older workers, or indeed to recognize what an immense social and economic resource they represent, both within and beyond the world of paid work.

There is mixed experience to draw upon, much of it connecting directly with the enormous resources and potential of occupational pension funds, and of state directed systems of the build up of pension entitlements. This is not simply a matter of preaching flexibility in the management of such schemes: for example, in face of organizational and structural change in public services, or the intense pressures of business cycles in industry and commerce — though there is much to be learnt from recent practice here. There are also significant issues of workers' rights, of the trustee responsibilities involved, and of issues of discrimination. Besides all this, there is a great deal to be gained from treating the transition from full-time work to active and creative "retirement" as being as important and complex for the individual and society as the transition of our young people into paid work. Rising life expectancy should have transformed perception of the resource and contribution of older people, as well as leading to a reconstruction of their needs.

For here, looking forward from the older workers' viewpoint, our categories do not have to be dominated by full-time paid work, nor by the dependence of incomes on such work. Creativity, experienced judgement, continued capacity for development, commitment, and acceptence of social responsibilities — how may all these be constructively developed? Because only part of the activity and contribution may be caught by the cash nexus and reflected in purported figures of "national wealth" is not a reason for neglecting the older generations in a discussion of European development. Rather, it is a reason for rethinking what we should be measuring, and how we should be measuring and understanding social and economic activity of many kinds, and on a vast scale. This should become an era in Europe noted for its creative voluntary activity and organization — a whole "third sector" (beyond and besides commercial-profit-based activity and the public sectors) of immense importance for our quality of life, community involvement and welfare, and for participatory democracy in its many forms.

So the Commission should cease to be old fashioned and restricted in its thinking, and actively engage in the grasp of the best practice and the change in all the categories of our thinking and response.

To start with the older workers. There are already very significant changes in economic activity rates, now palpable in the 50-59 age group, as more flexibility in retirement — or scaling down working time — becomes apparent from both the demand and the supply side. Most of this has not been built on longer term and humane concerns, not centred on the interests of the people concerned at this stage of their development, but arising out of the exigencies of organizational needs, and the pressures of depressed labour markets. But much has changed, and much has been learnt. What is needed is a more systematic attempt to review the use of pension funds in particular, (and state financial support) to handle retirement over a wider age range, to strengthen the rights of pension fund members in this process, to link state strategies with occupational funded provision. Besides, there should be strong encouragement, in the context of severe unemployment, of a variety of arrangements for reduced working time in the transition to full retirement, but without undermining or reducing final pension entitlement. "Final salary" schemes need to be adapted to encourage, instead of inhibiting, development of job sharing, part-time work in other forms, and so on, and access to longer paid and unpaid leave in later working life.

It is, then, crucial that pension fund resources — which, when "funded" may well build up financial resources greater than the existing and narrowly drawn minimum scheme entitlements — should not be dissipated or withdrawn by employers through failure in trusteeship (Maxwell), nor through exploitive attempts to capture and remove such "surpluses" as arise. In the UK we have recently witnessed companies asserting their "ownership" of the funds by not only stopping employer contributions, but by transferring funds back to the company. Take-overs have been, in some cases, connected with such exploitive interests, and we now have the UK Government coming forward with proposed extraction of vast sums from the coal and rail pension funds in the context of "privatization" — indeed, it seems to be a prime motive for privatizing since the organizational ideas destroy coherence and integration (rail), or encourage short-run exploitation of resources that could be tapped for the long run with new extraction techniques (coal). The European Community should seek to establish a wide and constructive consensus about workers' rights and pension fund responsibilities, not least since varying degrees of fiscal privilege have been provided for such funds.

Of course, the key principle of "equal opportunities" is also significant here. This is being approached in a very mechanical way — for example, to "meet" the equal opportunity requirement by moving to the least advantageous treatment for both sexes. It would be useful, instead, to have a wide and open European debate as to how equal treatment can be combined with recognition of the variety of people's needs and circumstances (importantly, with earlier access to pensions as a response to ill health). It is time the Commission developed a constructive programme that might lead on from urgent analysis and review of the many issues involved in retirement, to the issuing of some influential "opinions", and to Directives, not least on rights and trusteeship in pension funds. Besides, the Social Charter now needs extending from a too narrow concern with those in paid work to a positive support for the world of voluntary activity and responsible unpaid work. Where is Europe's "carers' charter" for the many millions of people who are contributing without reward to the care of others?

A fresh start

This is only the beginning of the agenda that is needed for a fresh start on a development programme directed at working people, their needs, and their actual and potential contribution. There are many other aspects that have a great significance. All too little has been done to meet the difficulties posed by increasing numbers of "self-employed"; the health and safety aspects of this may be where to take matters up afresh. Certainly the working time restrictions of the Working Time Directive must be fully enforceable in the case of the self-employed, or there will be yet another motive for employers to manipulate the employment status of many of their workers, as so many already have, to avoid legislative responsibilities.

The role of the public sector should also be emphasized. Governments, in the face of high unemployment, should be emphasizing the scope for shorter working hours (curtailing or eliminating overtime), and work-sharing in the public sector; such an emphasis barely exists at present. It is important, too, that the Commission has intervened to insist on full respect for the Transfer of Engagements Directive. The UK Government has been, for far too long, using the process of competitive tendering, with private sector bidders dissolving away the framework of full-time work and mutual responsibility established through collective bargaining. The irony is that such exploitive and low wage substitution costs the public finances more — not less — since it was designed to reduce both incomes and national insurance contributions (thus reducing public revenues). Beyond all this, attention should be given to signalling the social cost of practices of persistent overtime working, by raising the revenue levied on employers and workers concerned (possibly by a surcharge on national insurance, or its equivalent). These might reasonably be offset by waiving such costs on employers and employees for additional time spent in training within the basic working time pattern.

The final point to be made is that countries seeking to join the European Community should be committed to full acceptance of the Social Charter, and to adhesion to the stronger platform of application of the Charter set out in the Maastricht protocol. Responsible regulation of working time, and constructive labour market policies, are obviously part of what is required. The UK's aberrant behaviour in social policy has to be isolated, and to have no followers elsewhere.

CHAPTER 12

Afterword: An Assize on Unemployment and Poverty?

Ken Coates MEP

Britain enjoyed something very close to full employment for more than twenty-five years after the Second World War. Those who are old enough may well remember angry demonstrations outside the House of Commons when the total of unemployed rose above six hundred thousand. It became a popular assumption among psephologists that no Government would be electable if it allowed unemployment to surpass the three per cent level.

Today's conventional wisdom all runs the other way. Innumerable well-heeled apologists are pleased to tell us that full employment is quite impossible. Spin-doctors in all the political Parties focus their members' attention on those who remain in employment, and studiously ignore all others. Misery, alienation, narcotics and crime proliferate, while eminent political leaders announce that "there is no such thing as society". In the absence of society, of course, social responsibility evaporates. All misfortunes are henceforward the result of individual improvidence, fecklessness, caprice.

At the level of the economy, however, no one doubts the social dimension.

Rising productivity ensures a continual reduction in the demand for labour. With steady investment in advanced new machines, each year would produce the same output with less labour. It has been estimated that over recent decades this annual growth has reduced labour demand by something between two and three per cent in each average year. This increment, if it existed on Mars, might have been used to increase the availability of scarce goods, so that more people should benefit. But if the market on Mars were sated, then it would surely be used to maximize leisure.

But is that not indeed what is happening in Europe? Leisure is certainly increased, as the dole queues lengthen. Unfortunately, the burden of work on those who are not unemployed is then frequently intensified. In Britain, it was recently revealed that eighty million hours of overtime are worked each year, something under half of which are unpaid. That is to say, the equivalent of two million jobs are removed from the labour market by excessive working, and almost one million of these confiscated jobs go unremunerated. If the Martians had a word of advice for us, it would surely be: "share". How can we countenance such an unfair burden of work, and such an unfair burden of compulsory idleness?

Such a choice is only thinkable when the bonds of society have been stretched far too thin. What kind of "community" can exist then?

There is a secular commitment to better behaviour, in the United Nations Universal Declaration of Human Rights. This affirms, among all the other basic rights, the right to work. There are other commitments in the European Community: its founding Treaty insists on the maintenance of full employment. But there are also deeper commitments, with profound cultural roots.

The Labour movement was echoing these commitments, when it inscribed on its banners the motto "All for one and one for all". This was only a modern way of insisting that I am my brother's keeper, and that "inasmuch as ye have done this to the least of these My brethren, ye have done it unto Me".

The unemployed are the excluded people. They are excluded from all but the most essential markets, so that their want spills into the economic system to multiply a greater want, curtailing demand, and closing weaker enterprises. Dearth then rules. They are excluded from the sense of identity that is involved in making a needed contribution to the social good. In this exclusion seeds a powerful frustration, even antagonism. Allowed full nurture, this is profoundly discouraging: in a word, alienating. It may turn to suicide, or it may spurt into various forms of crime. Along the way, it breaks up homes, and fractures lives. Thus, these victims are excluded, by successive degrees, from one humane linkage after another.

To will a cure for this great plague of adversities, we must of course choose rational forms of political action. In modern Europe, this implies joint action, by all the states of the European Community, co-ordinated and urged forward by their common institutions. But how can we set such action free? That is the overpowering question of the day. There are millions of unemployed workers, and their families bring further millions to the legions of those who suffer. But there are millions of others, still at work, still aware of our common humanity, still unwilling to accept the division of Europe entailed in the creation of a tormented underclass, in, but not of, our own community.

It is time for all these millions to find their voices. The question is, what precisely to do?

Might we not call an assembly of concerned people? The form chosen for such a gathering might be an Assize, which has the connotation of some sort of convention, but also has a kind of legal penumbra. It will be remembered that an important assize was held in Rome during the preparation of the Maastricht summit. We could have an Assize on social cohesion, unemployment and poverty. There are innumerable professional organizations, voluntary bodies, and specialist agencies that have gathered considerable knowledge in these areas. Important experience has been acquired by the Churches, which now have expert groups concerned with "social responsibility" in the Anglican Church, and with "The World of Work" among Roman Catholics. Scholars and victims can testify to the depth of the gathering crisis in our community.

An assize need not be confined to a carefully structured enquiry in Brussels. It could range from Portugal to Germany, and from Denmark to Sicily, mobilizing, in the gathering of evidence, something of the range of popular disquiet. It could report, on local and national media, the extent and variety of the problems that mass unemployment has generated. It could stimulate the commitment for effective action in villages and suburban areas, in declining industries and deprived regions, but also in those zones of comfort and contentment that survive the blizzards raging all around.

It could interrogate the Commission and the various national authorities on their present proposals to meet the problems. And it could seek the responses of political Parties and other responsible organizations.

Is this not a labour for the Commission of the European Communities to make its own?

Elf Books

The Social Charter and the Single European Market
John Hughes

With wide-ranging developments and changes set in motion in the course of constructing the single European market, the needs of equity require a rapid evolution of new norms of social and political principle and practice to give substance to the Social Charter.

cloth 0 85124 523 4 £20.00
paper 0 85124 524 2 £6.95

European Union: Fortress or Democracy?
Michael Barratt Brown

Where is the way forward for economic and political development in the East and the South, as they relate to the whole of Europe, and how are we to overcome the plan-versus-market syndrome?

cloth 0 85124 520 X £20.00
paper 0 85124 521 8 £7.95

Against a Rising Tide
Racism, Europe and 1992
Mel Read MEP & Alan Simpson

1992 will bring enormous upheavals. How will it affect black people in Britain? The authors offer pratical ways in which local people can combat racism, setting their work in a European context.

cloth 0 85124 525 0 £20.00
paper 0 85124 526 9 £6.95

Whatever Happened to the Peace Dividend?
The Post-Cold War Armaments Momentum
Marek Thee

A new arms race was underway before the Gulf War. The author sets out the global drive for new high-tech weapons after the War, and makes clear why Europe's arms industry must plan its own conversion.

cloth 0 85124 532 3 £20
paper 0 85124 533 1 £7.95

Europe *Can* Afford to Work
Francis Cripps & Terry Ward

Economic growth is crucial to restoring employment in Europe's regions, as this book makes clear.

cloth 0 85124 551 x £25
paper 0 85124 550 1 £4.95

SPOKESMAN

Bertrand Russell House, Gamble Street, Nottingham NG7 4ET.
Tel: (0602) 708318